# Thinking
## LIKE A
# Lawyer

Critical thinking is the essential tool for ensuring that students fulfill their promise. But, in reality, critical thinking is still a luxury good, and students with the greatest potential are too often challenged the least. This best-selling book:

- Introduces a powerful but practical framework to close the critical thinking gap.
- Gives teachers the tools and knowledge to teach critical thinking to all students.
- Empowers students to tackle 21st-century problems.
- Teaches students how to compete in a rapidly changing global marketplace.

Colin Seale, a teacher-turned-attorney-turned-education-innovator and founder of thinkLaw, uses his unique experience to introduce a wide variety of concrete instructional strategies and examples that teachers can use in all grade levels. Individual chapters address underachievement, the value of nuance, evidence-based reasoning, social-emotional learning, equitable education, and leveraging families to close the critical thinking gap. In addition to offering examples for Math, Science, ELA, and Social Studies, this timely, updated second edition adds a variety of new examples and applications for Physical Education, Fine Arts, Foreign Language, and Career and Technical Education.

**Colin Seale** is an educator, attorney, and critical thinking expert. He founded thinkLaw, an award-winning organization, to help educators leverage inquiry-based instructional strategies that can close the critical thinking gap and ensure they teach and reach all students. Follow Colin on X (formerly Twitter) at @ColinESeale.

# Thinking
## LIKE A
# Lawyer

A Framework for Teaching
Critical Thinking to All Students
Second Edition

Colin Seale

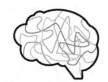

Routledge
Taylor & Francis Group

NEW YORK AND LONDON

Cover image: Allegra Denbo

Second edition published 2025
by Routledge
605 Third Avenue, New York, NY 10158

and by Routledge
4 Park Square, Milton Park, Abingdon, Oxon, OX14 4RN

*Routledge is an imprint of the Taylor & Francis Group, an informa business*

First edition published by Prufrock Press 2020

*Library of Congress Cataloging-in-Publication Data*
Names: Seale, Colin, 1982- author.
Title: Thinking like a lawyer : a framework for teaching critical thinking to all students / Colin Seale.
Description: Second edition. | New York, NY : Routledge, 2025. |
"First edition published by Prufrock Press 2020" – Title page verso. |
Includes bibliographical references.
Identifiers: LCCN 2024032214 (print) | LCCN 2024032215 (ebook) |
ISBN 9781032742274 (paperback) | ISBN 9781003482147 (ebook)
Subjects: LCSH: Critical thinking–Study and teaching. | Law–Study and teaching.
Classification: LCC LB1590.3 .S372 2025 (print) | LCC LB1590.3 (ebook) |
DDC 370.15/2–dc23/eng/20240715
LC record available at https://lccn.loc.gov/2024032214
LC ebook record available at https://lccn.loc.gov/2024032215

ISBN: 978-1-032-74227-4 (pbk)
ISBN: 978-1-003-48214-7 (ebk)

DOI: 10.4324/9781003482147

Typeset in Warnock Pro
by Deanta Global Publishing Services, Chennai, India

# Contents

# PART III
Practical Considerations for a Critical Thinking Revolution

# Acknowledgments

I dedicate this book to my mother, Ruth, for her relentless pursuit to get me to come somewhere close to fulfilling my potential. To my children, Rose and Oliver, for reminding me why I dream, and their mother Carrie whose partnership and flexibility has made this work possible. To the endless list of supportive family members, friends, colleagues, and mentors who always assure me that my dream is not crazy even when they secretly believe it is. To the members of thinkLaw's team in the past, present, and future whose dedication, passion, and expertise have poured all the nutrients we need into our garden for the bountiful harvest that is to come. To my co-conspirators in school systems who have transformed my dream of sparking a critical thinking revolution into a reality. Finally, I dedicate this to all of my former students who always taught me more than I taught them.

# Introduction

I have never been student of the month, the week, or even the day. I had 80 absences my freshman year in high school. I nearly dropped out of college, twice. But I graduated at the top of my law school class while teaching full time as a math teacher at a Title I school in Las Vegas, NV. Even more surprisingly, of the entire eighth grade class that I taught while in law school (do not try that at home), 74% of my students—who became Socratic masters and prolific problem solvers—scored proficient or higher on their state exam. This number was equal to or higher than the highest performing schools in the most affluent neighborhoods in the city. This book is about the power of leveraging the same practical "Thinking Like a Lawyer" strategies I used as a teacher and law student to fend off underachievement. More importantly, this book makes the case for a new guiding philosophy behind the purpose of education: unleashing the full critical thinking potential of all students.

In the five years prior to writing the first edition of this book, I obsessed over one question: *why don't we teach critical thinking to all students?* My journey to find answers was not an exercise in mere curiosity, but an urgent search for a missing piece in the education equity conversation. When education leaders discuss important challenges like stopping the school-to-prison pipeline, addressing chronic absenteeism, and ending racial disparities in academic performance, the national conversation

1

DOI: 10.4324/9781003482147-1

almost always revolves around closing the achievement gap. But what if educators focused on shattering achievement ceilings instead?

In the five years since, the global pandemic has only deepened these issues. We learned about the deep challenges so many students faced when it came to accessing technology and connecting to high-speed internet. But we still struggle to face the reality that so many students still lack access to challenging, meaningful grade-level content and still have no connection to the type of learning experiences that could spark their interest and excitement.

We all appreciate those moments when, even with all of our formal education, leadership roles, and professional experiences, we make a profound point to our colleagues on Zoom and realize that we forgot to turn off the mute button. Five years into the normalization of virtual meetings and this still happens? There's nothing like the moment of mutual relief and satisfaction when the sound issue has been resolved. It's so satisfying. Can you hear me now? Good!

Unfortunately, the actions and inactions of our educational systems prove that the true needs of our students are still muted. In the face of rising awareness of racial and social injustice in our nation and its impact on society, state legislatures decided to ban books and prohibit classroom discussion of very real historical and present issues. Since OpenAI launched ChatGPT in late 2022, artificial intelligence (AI) has exploded as a field with massive ramifications for revolutionizing the way we approach knowledge and knowing. And at the same time companies like Walmart[1] have introduced AI to large portions of their workforce (eliminating the need to have staff check receipts at Sam's Club stores by having an AI-powered video tool compare recently completed purchases to the items in a cart), some school districts chose to ban artificial intelligence altogether. These issues are all part of the same root problem.

After decades of reforms attempting to give every child access to rigorous educational opportunities, we are still not providing equitable access to deeper learning experiences. Critical thinking is at the heart of deeper learning, but in the scramble to close the achievement gap, we've created an unacceptable dichotomy. On one hand, critical thinking is the essential 21st-century skill. As a math-teacher-turned-attorney at one of Las Vegas's most prestigious law firms, I sat on the board for the Nevada STEM Coalition and led business conversations about the future of work and the urgent need to equip every student with critical thinking skills for our rapidly changing workforce. On the other hand, I saw a school system touting "proof" of its critical thinking efforts by showcasing magnet schools, career and technical academies, gifted and talented programs, and robotics and aviation afterschool programs for a handful of students. With the overwhelming majority of students excluded from these deeper learning opportunities, one thing was clear: critical thinking was and still is a luxury good.

This is the critical thinking gap, and this is not random. In classrooms, educators often stick to low-level questions because they do not believe critical thinking can be taught, do not believe it can be taught to all students, or do not believe in their own ability to teach critical thinking. Seeing is believing, so this is an issue of "how": how do we teach critical thinking, and how do we teach it to *all* students? Educators get little guidance on the "how" and struggle with a lack of training and tools to teach critical thinking unless they are part of the select few in elite academic programs. This gap increases for English language learners (ELLs), students who are academically behind their peers, or those receiving special education services. Often, even identified gifted students fall victim to this gap because of educators' misguided beliefs that "they will be just fine."

They will not be just fine. According to a 2007 study funded by the Jack Kent Cooke Foundation (Wyner et al., 2007), "although high achieving, low-income students tend to graduate from high school on time, they are more likely to attend less selective colleges than their more advantaged peers (21% vs. 14%), are less likely to graduate from college (49% vs. 77%), and are less likely to receive a graduate degree (29% vs. 47%)." Unfortunately, since the COVID-19 pandemic, these race and economic-based excellence gaps have grown even more (Coffey & Tyner, 2023). One in four high-achieving students from low-income backgrounds do not even take the SAT or ACT exam (Plucker et al., 2013). When we also consider the unacceptable fact that between 40% and 60% of students graduate from K–12 systems in need of college remediation (Jimenez et al., 2016), it becomes clear that we are leaving an incredible amount of genius on the table. With all this said, one conclusion is clear: the critical thinking gap is simply untenable.

We need a critical thinking revolution, and this revolution must be practical. Dynamic speakers at education conferences talk about the need to completely transform education. But if we are honest about what it will take to transition to a system with equitable access to deeper learning for all students, we must admit that this massive undertaking cannot succeed without an intensive and intentional classroom focus. This cannot succeed without practical strategies to work with, not around families. That is why this book exists.

*Thinking Like a Lawyer* is the how-to manual to unleash the critical thinking potential of all learners. This is the practical guide for designing classrooms that you would long for your own children to have. This is not some pie-in-the-sky fairy tale that you could only accomplish with lots of special technology, expensive makerspaces, and "high-performing" students. This is the practical critical thinking guide for all teacher leaders, including the ones at the one-room schoolhouse, the juvenile detention education center, and the "we've got everything" magnet school. For educators teaching students who are still struggling with the very real challenge of pandemic-related learning loss, this book is a map for not meeting students where they are, but guiding them to where they need to be by using critical thinking as the lever for defying the drill-and-kill process of remediation.

No revolution can happen without a healthy dose of propaganda. That's why Part I of this book's powerful, but practical critical thinking revolution is all about evangelism. This section features my testimony as a recovering underachiever, defines and pushes the definition of what critical thinking actually is (and why it's so hard to teach), and highlights practical examples to show why the critical thinking gap is the most crucial equity issue in education no one is talking about. This is not about a liberal or conservative view of education. It's not a so-called "woke" or white supremacist agenda. This is about our power to create everyday, sustainable classroom opportunities for young people to transform their lives through education.

Part II gets into the nitty-gritty of the Thinking Like a Lawyer method (thinkLaw for short), with practical guidance for leveraging our students' inherent sense of justice and fairness as a hook for unleashing their critical thinking potential. This section uses real-life examples of hilarious, absurd, and did-that-really-happen-for-real legal cases to highlight engaging and rigorous frameworks for developing critical thinking skills and dispositions. Each powerful thinkLaw strategy—like analysis from multiple perspectives, mistake analysis, and investigation and discovery—is followed by detailed practical applications for all grade levels and multiple subject areas. In the first edition of this book, the examples were limited to the core subjects of Math, Science, English Language Arts, and Social Studies. The second edition includes examples and applications for Physical Education, Fine Arts, Foreign Language, and Career and Technical Education.

Lastly, Part III discusses the practical implications of adopting the thinkLaw framework. All the strategies in the world are meaningless without addressing the very real implementation barriers that make any instructional change difficult. Part III works through this difficulty by helping educators scaffold for critical thinking, ensuring that these rigorous, deeper learning experiences can be accessible for all students. This section also includes concrete tools to support practical lesson planning considerations to ensure that your critical thinking lesson that looks amazing on paper does not fall apart in practice. Then, I challenge the notion of student engagement for engagement's sake and make a case for refining engagement with a much more intentional focus on deeper learning.

This section also connects these thinkLaw strategies to two issues that teachers are forced to care about across the board: classroom management and student performance on standardized exams. And because parents and families are the most important teachers in the lives of learners, this section also includes powerful strategies for families to use at home. The changes schools need in order to unleash critical thinking skills and dispositions will be improbable and unsustainable if we do not involve our students' families. By the end of this book, readers will have the practical tools needed to build a world where critical thinking is no longer a luxury good. Welcome to the critical thinking revolution!

# Note

1  https://blogs.microsoft.com/blog/2024/01/09/walmart-unveils-new -generative-ai-powered-capabilities-for-shoppers-and-associates/

# PART I

## Closing the Critical Thinking Gap

# Chapter 1

# The Autobiography of a Recovering Underachiever

I struggle with telling the story of my childhood. When I talk about the challenges of growing up in a single-parent, immigrant household with a father who was incarcerated for a decade because of drug trafficking, my story sounds like one of those "despite all odds" clichés that ignore an important reality: my success story (like those of so many children who grew up like me) is a story based on "because," not "despite."

I was born in November, but I was a child who needed to defy birth month requirements for starting school. My mother did whatever testing I needed to make sure she did not have to wait another year for me to start kindergarten. I do not remember much about my half-day kindergarten experience, but I was not a well-behaved boy. I distinctly remember loving the book *Caps for Sale* (Slobodkina, 1968) so much that I would throw epic fits when my teacher decided to read a different book during story time. The only sin greater than reading the wrong book was choosing to read *Caps for Sale* the wrong way. If my teacher refused to yell, "Caps! Caps for sale. Fifty cents a cap" in an extra loud voice with a generically European accent (which was likely pretty offensive in retrospect), I found it necessary to run up to her and smack the book out of her hands.

When my parents separated, and I moved in with my grandmother in Crown Heights, Brooklyn, my struggles became more real. I was in

DOI: 10.4324/9781003482147-3

trouble constantly, and my early elementary school version of trouble was a special type. For example, I had trouble with a science lab teacher named Ms. Liftshitz, who used to push into our classes (but, really, how could I not get in trouble when my science teacher had that name?). Ms. Liftshitz once made me write a 100-word reflection on my behavior. So, I thought about it, did the math in my head, and decided to write, "I hate science" 32 times so I would have four words left over to write, "I hate you, too."

These behaviors did not come out of nowhere. I was a fluent reader before kindergarten and already knew a ton of math. I sat in class almost every day, and the same routine happened: the teacher covered material I already knew, so I talked to other students and got in trouble. She gave out classwork I would finish in two minutes, and then I would talk to other students and get in trouble. Then, as a consequence, she would give me more work—not harder or more challenging work, just more. So, the cycle continued.

Around that time, a caring teacher's aide let my mother know that I needed to get tested. My mom probably figured that something was wrong with me, but it turned out that the aide wanted me to be tested to see if I should be receiving gifted and talented services. These services were not offered at my school, or even in my district. This was single-handedly the most important event of my K–12 school career.

When I tested into gifted programming and started school at P.S. 208 as part of a self-contained gifted and talented class in the district's Astral program, everything changed. I transferred in after the school year had already started. On my first day, there was a word on the chalkboard—something like "green." I looked around and saw that everyone was writing in their black-and-white composition books. Confused, I asked the student next to me, "Hey, where's the worksheet? What are we supposed to be doing?" He looked at me like I was clueless. "This is creative writing time," he said. "You just write. Write about 'green'."

This was exactly the transformation I needed. Now, I was expected to get out of my seat and talk to my peers. Now, I was required to question my teacher. Now, almost every assignment was even more exciting than reading *Caps for Sale* because we were writing and illustrating our own fairy tales. We had a math lab elective in second grade before STEM and STEAM were a thing. But because even engaging curriculum and rigorous learning environments could not contain my unique brand of shenanigans, I still got put out of class quite often for acting up.

Getting put out of class opened my eyes to education inequity for the first time. It turned out that although my gifted class only had 24 students, the other classes in my school had more than 30. What struck me even harder was that every class I got sent to had at least a handful of students that reminded me of *me*. They were getting in lots of trouble, but it seemed like the work also came too easy for them. The biggest kicker for me was that, in the second grade, classes just included second graders. The third grade classes just had third graders. But my gifted class was a bridge class with second and third graders. In this Title I school that we gifted students were bussed to, educators could only find 12 students per grade level to access this transformational educational experience.

Reflecting on this inequity helped me realize a guiding principle of my mission in education: brilliance is distributed equally, but too often, opportunity is not. There was also another crucial takeaway I would not understand for decades. In this class full of 24 non-White gifted learners, three of these rock star students would not graduate high school—and I was almost the fourth.

I almost became the fourth even though I was the best eighth grader an eighth grader could ever be. My classmates and I remained isolated in our gifted programs throughout middle school except for gym class and lunch. Our team of sixth-grade teachers saw something in us and made the unprecedented decision to start us in New York City's equivalent of Algebra I in the seventh grade. By the time I was ready to walk in my eighth-grade promotion ceremony, I was double accelerated in math and English, had high school credits for French, and was in the National Honor Society. Any time my middle school leadership needed to put on a dog and pony show, I was appointed to be the dog and the pony. Then, all of a sudden, I just stopped caring.

I was afflicted with "I don't care" syndrome. I was the only person from my junior high school to attend the prestigious Bronx High School of Science, and I was not too keen about traveling 90 minutes each way from Brooklyn to the Bronx. And I definitely did not love the transition from my almost all-Black elementary and middle schools to a school where non-White and non-Asian students were well under 15% of the student population.

I went months without turning in homework assignments because, for some reason, no one raised any concerns about going months without turning in homework assignments. I was an African American male slacker at the same high school that graduated eight Nobel Prize winners, six Pulitzer Prize winners, and Neil deGrasse Tyson. And because I decided to take lunch during every single lunch period, I ended the year with more than 80 class absences and either failed or barely passed most of my classes. No one intervened.

The truth was, this school was hard—but not in the engaging way my elementary and junior high schools had been. Those schools had challenged and sparked my curiosity about just about everything. Instead, it felt like this school was just hard for the sake of being hard. In ninth-grade global studies, we had to watch *Gandhi* and answer a ton of questions from a worksheet. My mom came back from the library with the two-VHS set, and I looked at these videos, trying to figure out why any teacher would expect me to take time out of my precious teenage weekend to watch this three-hour-and-eleven-minute movie about a dude I'd known about since elementary school. This was precisely the type of assignment I simply did not care to do, and an example of the type of assignments this "hard" school kept on asking me to do.

What brought me out of the funk of underachievement was one adult who refused to let me waste my potential. Ms. Simon, a counselor, pulled me into her office. I had always thought she was just a mean lady because she looked like she could have been one of those gruff detectives from *Law & Order* in another lifetime. But Ms. Simon showed me that she cared about me by pulling out my old middle school records and telling me she believed I had more potential than I was demonstrating. Rather than scolding me about skipping classes or giving me heavy-handed consequences, she gave me the option of carrying around an attendance sheet to each of my classes as a voluntary accountability measure to help me own my skipping issues. Ms. Simon made it her business to ensure I did not become another tragedy of wasted potential.

To graduate on time, I had to go to summer school after my junior year. I ended up attending Dewitt Clinton High School right down the street from Bronx Science because my school was under construction. There, I had another awakening. My love affair with every lunch period forced me to take art that summer, and I took it with a class full of Clinton students who also failed art during the school year. But something strange happened. When the teacher found out I went to Bronx Science, she said out loud, "You must be really, really smart." She did not know anything about my struggles, so even though I was generally awful at art, I felt like I had to keep the gig up. We had to make a sculpture out of a bar of soap, and I remember spending a whole weekend (triple the time it would've taken me to watch *Gandhi*) designing this intricate sunrise sculpture that blew the teacher's mind. She reminded me of the power of belief: because she unequivocally believed I was capable of excellence, I believed it, too.

After this, I just kept up the act until it seemed I did not have to act anymore. I realized how to play the game and started to play it. My grades skyrocketed, I was able to qualify for advanced placement courses, and I honestly started to love being a Bronx Science student. I decided to do the thing that made sense for anyone who graduated in 2000 in the height of the dot-com bubble: major in computer science.

It did not matter that I had not written a line of code in my life. It did not even matter that I had no clue whether I liked anything about computer science. As the first generation of my family in this country, if I could just graduate and get a good job at Microsoft, I was going to give my mom all sorts of bragging rights. I was likely motivated by an interesting mathematical analogy Neil deGrasse Tyson made at our graduation to help us understand his excitement about being in the "era of nerds" by explaining how rich Bill Gates was. Tyson explained that, given his own role and salary at the time, if he were walking down the street and saw a penny, he would ignore it. He'd probably also ignore a nickel. A dime he would have to think about, but there's no way Tyson wasn't going to pocket a quarter. Using this same unit of analysis, it would not make sense for Bill Gates to stop to pick up $10,000. In other words, it was time for me to get paid!

But my dreams of a multibillionaire lifestyle as a tech titan were put on pause the first day of my computer lab course. It appeared that I was one of the few students who had absolutely no coding experience before deciding to major in computer science. So, before I could figure out how to turn my computer on, at least ten of my colleagues finished the lab, laughing on their way out about how easy the assignment was. I looked down at my assignment, looked at the blank computer screen, and by the time I scratched my head a few times trying to figure out what seemed like hieroglyphics, almost every student was out of the lab. I started to feel so discouraged because I was smart, right? The art teacher said so, my family members said so, and many teachers had told me so when I was younger. If I was so smart, why couldn't I do this? Maybe I'm actually not smart at all? By the time I finished having this conversation in my head, the graduate assistant came up to me and asked me if I was finished. That's when I realized there was no one left in the lab but the two of us. I looked at the lab assignment I did not understand. I looked at my blank computer screen.

And I said, "Yes. I'm done." That was the moment I almost dropped out of college.

I cried all of the way back to my dorm. When I got to my room, I immediately called my mom, crying about how someone needed to come and take me home because I had no idea what I was doing. Looking back, I do not remember what I expected my mom to say in response to any of this. I scored in the 99th percentile for every single state math assessment I took until sixth grade, when I scored in the 95th percentile, and my mom asked me, "What happened to those other four points?" My mom was really not the go-to person for these types of conversations, but she's all I had. But this time, my mom channeled her inner Carol Dweck and reminded me that my success had less to do with being smart and much more to do with persevering. She told me, "You have always figured things out, and you just have to figure this out. I have to go back to work." So, she went back to work. And so did I. I sat in my professor's office hours at least once a week to work through stuff I did not understand. I thought the final project was boring, so I designed a program that incorporated my love of music. The program out-putted the notes for chords a musician could play based on the notes in a song. I earned an A in the class that had almost become the reason I dropped out of college.

When you read these experiences, and then learn that I ended up being president of the student association at Syracuse University, the keynote speaker for the university's first ever African American Student Graduation, an early admit to the Maxwell School of Citizenship and Public Affairs (the nation's top program for public administration) complete with full tuition and a stipend for expenses to complete this one-year program, and later a gap-closing math educator, child welfare reformer, and award-winning attorney at one of the nation's most prestigious corporate law firms before launching a revolutionary education organization that has exploded across the nation, it is tempting to categorize this as a certain type of victory: succeeding "despite" the obstacles.

But my story, like the stories of so many other students who overcome barriers, is really about the "because." Because my mother had to make a dollar out of 15 cents, optimize constraints, and leverage resources, people, and systems in any way she could to raise two children as a single mother, I have an endless sense of possibility. "Because, not despite" is a powerful lens for educators to view gaps between potential and performance. English language learners have a massive competitive advantage for academic excellence because, not despite the fact that they spend so much time thinking and navigating across multiple languages and cultures. Struggling learners have the building blocks for tremendous academic success, not despite their struggles, but because their learning challenges force them to become experts in learning how to learn. Creating a world where critical thinking is no longer a luxury good requires educators to recognize the inherent critical thinking potential of all students.

My journey as a recovering underachiever created the lens through which I am asking educators to see the world in this journey to close the critical thinking gap. All of the critical thinking tips and strategies in the world are meaningless if educators do not first believe that all students are capable of excellence. Even when that belief is there, educators need to go further by making it their business to ensure that we no longer have so many tragedies of wasted potential. We simply have to stop leaving genius on the table.

# Chapter 2

# Defining Critical Thinking

What is critical thinking? When I travel across the country training educators for thinkLaw, I always ask this question. Inevitably, teachers provide answers with the preface "the ability to" or "being able to" do a wide variety of skills. Thinking outside the box, synthesizing information, supporting claims with evidence, and analyzing issues from multiple perspectives are some of the most common responses.

I have also asked this question to thousands of students across the United States. Because kids are kids, they frequently give the brilliant response, "Critical thinking is thinking critically." Occasionally, students say that critical thinking is when you're thinking about ways to criticize other people. But one student response stood out more than any other: "Critical thinking is what teachers never let us do in school."

## Critical Thinking Skills and Dispositions

Often, educators think about critical thinking as a set of skills that only the most advanced students can handle. This student's comment reminded me of Romel, the sharpest young man I'd ever come across in my career as an educator. He was an amazing problem solver and a super creative

DOI: 10.4324/9781003482147-4

thinker. But here's the thing: Romel was not a student in my class, and his problem was not in math or science. Romel was my client in my law school's juvenile justice clinic, and his problem was trying to figure out how to beat adult charges after he'd been arrested on a serious drug bust just one month before his 18th birthday. Romel had unquestionable critical thinking skills that he leaned on every single day just to survive.

But critical thinking requires more than just skills. Students also need the mindsets and the habits to *apply* critical thinking skills *consistently* throughout life, academics, and career. These critical thinking dispositions (see Figure 2.1) are often the missing pieces to our working definition of critical thinking. All educators are intimately familiar with this, because we have all known that one person, child or adult, who is unquestionably brilliant, yet finds some way to do some of the stupidest things imaginable on a regular basis. (*Note.* If you don't know that person, it is very likely *you* might be the person I'm talking about.) The difference between knowing better and doing better is often explained by the gap between critical thinking skills and dispositions.

FIGURE 2.1
*Critical Thinking Skills and Dispositions Applied Across Contexts*

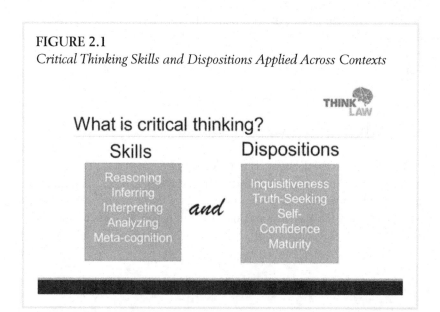

## Solving Problems Across Disciplines

A working definition is even more complex because even when students have the skills and dispositions, critical thinking tends to be extremely context-dependent. How often do students who rock it out in math show little or no willingness to apply the slightest effort in writing? Why is it common for students to love the fine arts so much that they can observe and analyze a painting for hours but shut down immediately when using similar observation skills to figure out what's causing a chemical reaction to occur in science class? Futurist Alvin Toffler pointed out that "the illiterate of the 21st century will not be these who cannot read or write. It will be those who cannot learn, unlearn, and relearn" (as cited in Subramanian, 2016, para. 7). Educators must be in the business of teaching critical thinking skills and dispositions in a way that transfers across disciplines (see Figure 2.2).

"Learning how to learn" does not mean that all our students need is surface-level knowledge. Nor does it mean that there is no place for rote

FIGURE 2.2
*Critical Thinking Skills and Dispositions Applied Across Contexts and Framed Around the Idea that Doing Right Is More Important than Being Right*

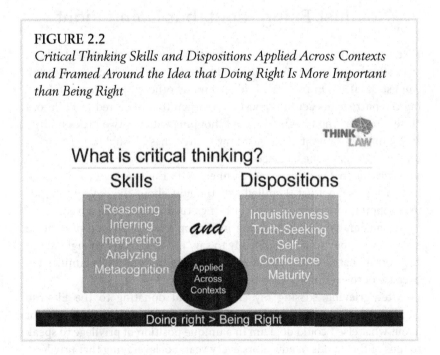

memorization whatsoever. It is outrageous to suggest that a fourth grader can develop the number sense needed to understand exponents without a thorough content mastery of multiplication. It is similarly challenging to analyze the major themes in *The Scarlet Letter* with any meaningful depth without knowing the historical context of this novel and referencing similar prosecutions of women in the past like the Salem witch trials. An educator's goal, then, must be to equip students with the navigational and inquiry tools they need to learn how to learn and apply this learning across disciplines.

Applying critical thinking across contexts is a key consideration in the growing debate about what level of content knowledge is needed to think critically about a subject. This is where the dispositions of inquisitiveness and maturity become particularly important. The wisest scholars are those who have the awareness to understand what they do not know and the truth-seeking impulse to thoroughly investigate questions to reach a workable depth of content knowledge.

## Not Just Being Right, but Doing Right

Last, but certainly not least, students must have worthy objectives to think critically about. To highlight this point, I want to think back to Saturday, August 3, 2019. On this day, I, like so many others, spent hours following the outrageous act of domestic terrorism that occurred in El Paso. I closed my eyes and imagined school shopping with my two little children at Walmart. I thought about just how many times I would have to say no to my daughter as she leveraged her greatest negotiation tactics to get me to buy items that were even more unnecessary than some of the items on her back-to-school list. I smiled as I thought about the reality that, for us, shopping for the most basic of things turns into a long adventure of exploring random aisles, running into people we know, and presenting even more opportunities for Daddy to say "no." But then I thought about the horror that so many of the witnesses, victims, and their families felt because of the actions of the domestic terrorist.

After grieving, kissing my children, and donating to the El Paso Community Foundation to help victims and their families, I thought about what else I could do. I am in a unique position of privilege to speak to tens of thousands of educators every year. So, leveraging that privilege,

I've decided to own up to the shortcomings of my work in the hopes that educators can also come to accept this truth: critical thinking, in and of itself, is not enough.

The limitations of critical thinking are not new. While attending Morehouse College, Dr. Martin Luther King Jr. (1947) rightfully noted the problems with an education focused on mere intellectual pursuits: "The most dangerous criminal may be the man gifted with reason, but with no morals" (p. 10). This serves as the preface to one of his more famous quotes: "Intelligence plus character—that is the goal of true education." It is easy to read these words and conclude that what's missing from critical thinking is a more intense focus on character education, but Dr. King's point is much bigger.

Dr. King (1947) further explained that "the complete education gives one not only power of concentration, but worthy objectives upon which to concentrate" (p. 10). Education is not complete just because we give students the tools to analyze the way the world is. It is complete if, and only if, we equip students with the tools they need to question the way the world *ought to be*. It is complete if, and only if, we reject the myth of objectivity—the myth that says it is inappropriate for educators to be political. Education is inherently political. Silence at important moments speaks volumes. Students hear this silence loud and clear.

I am not advocating for teachers to indoctrinate students. I am expressly acknowledging, however, the limitations of the thinkLaw critical thinking framework in which we ask students to make claims supported by valid and relevant evidence, analyze issues from multiple perspectives, weigh consequences, and draw conclusions based on this analysis. Because the truth is, not every issue requires this level of nuance.

We learn that 1 + 1 is 2 because it just is. And that 1 + 1 is not 3 because it just isn't. White supremacy is wrong. It just is. Hating people because of who they are, where they were born, or the color of their skin is wrong. It just is. Being silent in the face of hate and ignorance is wrong. It just is. Less than two years before the El Paso shooting, when the Unite the Right rally in Charlottesville, VA—a coming out party for the modern-day Ku Klux Klan with tiki torches instead of white hoods—led to tragedy, I issued a call to action to educators about the urgency of responding. But the response I call for is more than just "thoughts and prayers."

Dr. King's (1965) belief that "the arc of the moral universe is long, but it bends toward justice" was not simply a prayer. This belief was equal parts "pray like it all depends on God" and "work like it all depends on you."

The arc will not bend without direct action. Thus, direct action is needed to ensure hate, ignorance, and violence never become "worthy objectives upon which to concentrate" (King, 1947, p. 10).

So, as I refer to critical thinking throughout this book, I do so with the knowledge that part of my duty from this point on is to insist that closing the critical thinking gap is no longer enough. Sure, I want to make sure that powerful 21st-century skills are not reserved only for the most elite students at the most elite schools. But I also need to be clear: critical thinking is not enough without a clear focus on using it to dismantle hate and ignorance.

The idea that it is not enough for our students to *be* right, but that they must also *do* right is an essential part of 21st-century critical thinking. For example, Neil deGrasse Tyson is arguably the most important science intellectual of our time. I am slightly biased because he was not just a fellow alumnus of Bronx High School of Science, but was also the commencement speaker at my graduation. Between the success of his *Cosmos* television series and books like *Astrophysics for People in a Hurry*, he is not just a gifted man, but a man who can skillfully communicate complex topics to the masses.

I was appalled, however, to see him write the following tweet the day after the El Paso shooting, just hours after another mass shooting in Dayton, OH (Tyson, 2019):

> In the past 48hrs, the USA horrifically lost 34 people to mass shootings.
> On average, across any 48hrs, we also lose…
> 500 to Medical errors
> 300 to the Flu
> 250 to Suicide
> 200 to Car Accidents
> 40 to Homicide via Handgun
> Often our emotions respond more to spectacle than to data.

By pulling these numbers out and researching this data, it appears Tyson was "right." But what does technical correctness matter at a moment of national mourning? The fact that 500 people randomly die due to medical errors every 48 hours is correct, but should these random mistakes be compared to domestic terrorism? When a group of people are hunted down because of who they are while they are completing the innocent, commonplace act of going back-to-school shopping, it shatters the very nature of what it means to be safe. Being right is not as important as doing right, and this distinction matters.

A less serious example of this distinction happened a few months ago when I was washing dishes after dinner. My brilliant daughter was writing one of her lists (she has lists for everything) when I interrupted her planning to ask her to pass me a cup. Here's how the conversation went:

> **Me:** Can you pass me a cup, please?
>
> **My daughter:** Cup? I don't see a cup anywhere.
>
> **Me:** There's a cup right there in front of you. Pass me the cup so I can put it in the dishwasher.
>
> **My daughter:** Daddy, there is no cup. I see a *glass* though.

Honestly, I lost it at that point. The last thing I would ever want in this world is for my brilliant daughter to turn into one of those annoying people who know exactly what you are talking about but play dumb because of some small technicality. I made it clear that no one wants to be friends with people who make them feel stupid. To purposely make things difficult for someone who calls a drinking device a "cup" instead of a "glass" is simply not okay. It's more important to do right (i.e., pass the cup, glass, goblet, tumbler, etc.) than to be right.

To be clear, I am not arrogant enough to believe I can actually know what "doing right" really means. Nor do I believe that educators can define "doing right" for their students in every context. But I do know this: our world would be a much better place to live in if everyone understood and practiced a mantra of, "just because I can, doesn't mean that I should." The ability to differentiate between technical correctness and actual appropriateness is a crucial distinction our young people must grapple with to thrive in the world.

This crucial part of critical thinking often goes overlooked. There is a reason the public sentiment of anti-intellectualism is so strong. All of the knowledge and problem-solving abilities in the world mean nothing if the holder of this knowledge and ability is a jerk. Therefore, my expanded definition of critical thinking includes the distinction between being right and doing right, disagreeing without being disagreeable, and generally not being a jerk.

In summary, our working definition of critical thinking has four components. Critical thinking is:

1. the set of *skills* and *dispositions* we need
2. to *learn what we need to learn*
3. to *solve problems across disciplines*
4. that are *grounded in the spirit of doing right instead of simply being right.*

None of this should be considered groundbreaking information because this four-part definition of critical thinking is not a novel concept. Maybe this sounds familiar because your district focuses heavily on the six competencies of deeper learning—mastering core academic content, thinking critically and solving complex problems, working collaboratively, communicating effectively, learning how to learn, and developing academic mindsets—which look and feel very similar (The Hewlett Foundation, 2013). This shouldn't feel much different than Sandra Kaplan's Depth and Complexity Framework that focuses on deep understanding, "knowing the language, details, patterns, rules, trends, unanswered questions, ethics, and big ideas that make up a topic's content," and complex understanding, "examining the change in the topic over time, different perspectives of the topic, and how it connects to other disciplines" (The Center For Depth and Complexity, 2024).

It's possible that this definition conjures up tenets of social and emotional learning (SEL). The Collaborative for Academic, Social and Emotional Learning defines SEL as:

> the process through which all young people and adults
> acquire and apply the knowledge, skills, and attitudes to
> develop healthy identities, manage emotions and achieve
> personal and collective goals, feel and show empathy for
> others, establish and maintain supportive relationships,
> and make responsible and caring decisions.
>
> (CASEL, 2023)

Although SEL has recently been looked at with suspicion from a vocal minority of advocates who consider SEL part of a dangerous, so-called "woke" agenda in education, SEL—like critical thinking—is and has always just been a part of what good teaching looks like.

I experienced this in Owensboro, Kentucky, in July 2023 while in town preparing for a workshop with Daviess County Public Schools. In the birthplace of bluegrass music—hardly a bastion of bleeding-heart liberal politics—I felt goosebumps on my skin when I had the chance to visit the local library and listen to an interview of Grant Talbot III, a member of the first integrated class at Owensboro High School after segregation ended in 1962. Out of all of his inspirational stories about how his educational experiences during those trying times motivated his decision to become a school counselor in the same community, one pair of quotes stood out:

> "I got a good education... maybe not academically as much as I did about life and social aspects of living with people."
> "We were taught character. Those things that were right and wrong that carry on through life."[1]

The rallying cry some education advocates have for a back-to-basics approach to the three Rs of "reading, 'riting, and 'rithmetic" is based on a false sense of nostalgia. From the days of the one-room schoolhouse, the purpose of education has been more grounded in a different triplet of Rs: relationships, relevance, and rigor. In an education landscape plagued with change fatigue and professionals struggling with "one more thing" syndrome, it should come as a welcome relief to realize that there is no earth-shattering shift involved in prioritizing critical thinking. As school systems, state departments of education, and nations across the world have proclaimed the importance of critical thinking for their portraits and profiles of a graduate, it is helpful to recognize that this is not a new, innovative approach. But as the next chapter will discuss, it *is* a novel idea to ensure that critical thinking, in practice, is not treated like a luxury good.

# Note

1 III, Grant Talbot, interview by Daniel Hildenbrandt. May 12, 1999, Owensboro-Daviess County: Race Relations, 1930–1970 Oral History Project, Louie B. Nunn Center for Oral History, University of Kentucky Libraries.

# Chapter 3

# The Critical Thinking Gap

In my first few years of training educators across the country on powerful but practical critical thinking strategies, I found myself hearing a similar objection repeatedly. It did not matter whether I was working in large or small school systems, urban, rural, or suburban areas, or affluent or high-poverty communities. The objection I consistently heard had to do with students and their ability to think critically, a "can't, don't, and won't" issue: "Students *can't* think critically. They *don't* think critically. And if I use up my precious time as a busy educator to design lessons to unleash their critical thinking potential, they *won't* think critically."

This mindset highlights an unspoken agreement about who gets access to critical thinking instruction. Critical thinking often seems normal for educators teaching to the most "elite" students in our most "elite" schools. This is the critical thinking gap. This gap explains our tendency to limit critical thinking access to students attending rigorous learning academies or who are placed in Advanced Placement courses, the International Baccalaureate program, gifted and talented programs, or honors classes. But we are well past the point where we can afford for access to meaningful critical thinking instruction to be an honor.

If you step into the shoes of a college-bound twelfth grader, you would understand that five years from now, you will be entering a workforce where entire industries are booming that do not currently exist. At the

DOI: 10.4324/9781003482147-5

same time, industries that are booming right now may be completely wiped out in five years. Simply put, educators cannot afford to continue to treat critical thinking like a luxury good—not when it is such an essential 21st-century asset.

To be clear, this is not just about the future of work. Education's value extends far beyond the workforce. If we think of education as a path to ensure an active and engaged citizenry, how do we get there without critical thinking? The sheer quantity of information, matched with the vast amount of unreliable online sources, makes the process of determining the truth challenging. Additionally, social media algorithms tend to surround us with more of the viewpoints we agree with and make us less open to understanding different points of view. We have settled for a world where we deem it impolite to discuss politics or religion. As a result, we seem completely incapable of respectfully discussing politics and religion.

This gap is an important and urgent issue in the K–12 education system. Despite non-educators' common belief that teachers just "teach to the test," almost all high-stakes statewide assessments for math and English language arts are impossible to succeed on without critical thinking. Gone are the days of choosing simple fill-in-the-blank responses for problems that merely test skills and the ability to perform a concrete task, like solving an equation. Today's questions are more complex—requiring multiple steps, inferences, predictions, and careful judgments about which potential answer is best—and they are asked in a wide variety of unique formats.

But as important as standardized testing has become to school accountability, when I spoke to more than 300 educators to learn how the critical thinking gap impacted them, standardized testing rarely came up. What did come up? A school with lots of high-achieving students that ended up with ten valedictorians speaking at their commencement because their top students could not stop fighting over who should hold this honor. *Students cared more about grades and rankings than the process of learning itself.*

Speaking of fighting, several secondary educators spoke of their challenges with student disputes escalating to blows faster than ever, especially with young girls. In fact, I was once in a principal's office as she was reviewing our curriculum and expressing her excitement for how analyzing cases from multiple perspectives could help students improve their conflict resolution skills. At that exact moment, I heard a string of expletives followed by screaming, and the principal stormed out of her office.

Two girls fought right outside of the principal's front door. *Students struggled to disagree without being disagreeable, leading to damaging school culture.*

The impact of the critical thinking gap is clearly larger than academics. At the same time, the critical thinking gap is bigger than we think, even in programs for gifted and talented students. To start with, there are tremendous equity issues with the underrepresentation of African American, Latinx, ELL, and low-income student populations in gifted education. But even if we figured out equitable identification practices, there are still far too many gifted and talented programs across the country that are gifted in name only. Often, these programs are limited to pulling students out of their classes once or twice a week to receive gifted services in elementary school. This ignores the fact that gifted students are gifted all day long and fosters a "not my job" mentality for general education teachers.

Services for gifted and talented students fall even shorter in secondary grades. Despite a broad recognition that gifted learners are not necessarily high achievers, the vast majority of secondary services for gifted and talented students revolve around accelerated or advanced coursework. One study estimated that 5% of gifted and talented students drop out of high school (Ritchotte & Graefe, 2017), and one out of four high-achieving students from low-income backgrounds do not even apply to college (Plucker et al., 2013). This shows us that what we are doing for our best and brightest students simply is not working.

The impact of this broken system disproportionately hurts high-achieving, low-income students. These students may graduate from high school on time but are less likely to attend selective colleges, graduate from any college, or receive a graduate degree (Wyner et al., 2007). This issue is not limited to our highest-ability students. In a study focusing on the gap between potential and performance, 88% of high school dropouts interviewed had passing grades but dropped out due to boredom (Bridgeland et al., 2006). If our education system is not unleashing the full potential of the students we have identified as the best and the brightest, what does that mean for the rest of them?

I can rattle off even more numbers here. But numbers alone do not really tell the story of the negative impact of the critical thinking gap. Stories tell the story. I often recall a specific sixth grade classroom I visited where more than half of the students were reading a book because they had finished their work already. I quickly noticed that this was a classroom

of English language learners. The teacher herself had the firsthand experience of being an ELL as a child. But I was surprised when I looked at the
student worksheets and realized they were adding "ing" onto the end of
verbs. This was a sixth grade class, but the bottom of this worksheet indi-
cated that the worksheet was from a third grade textbook. When I asked
this teacher why her students were doing third grade work in the sixth
grade, she informed me that they were "very low" and "could not handle"
the grade-level work.

I have seen school leaders say "enough is enough" to these types of low
expectations. These school leaders often implement rigorous math and
English language arts curriculum across the board to ensure that students
are accessing challenging, grade-level work. One leader invested in expensive curricular resources and intense training and professional development for teachers to use this curriculum successfully. She was thrilled
that a teacher with excellent growth results from a nearby school serving
students who were from predominantly suburban, upper-middle-class
families was coming to her school, which served students from predominantly urban, high-poverty families. The rigor and critical thinking were
present in this curriculum, in theory. In one lesson I observed, students
had to analyze two pieces of text: one on the history of the traffic light
and another on the history of community barn-building. Then they had to
synthesize these texts to explain how these two practices contributed to
the development of communities. But here's the catch: this teacher drew a
huge X across the text about traffic lights. According to this teacher, these
students "could barely read" and "their writing was even worse," so it was
"impossible" to ask them to do the assignment as designed.

I agreed. It is impossible to expect students to be the critical thinkers
that the 21st century demands when educators guarantee that students
will not have access to critical thinking. According to TNTP's (2018)
groundbreaking report "The Opportunity Myth," stories like these are
more often the rule than the exception. TNTP concluded that students
from low-income backgrounds were successfully completing 71% of what
educators asked of them, but only 17% of the work they were asked to do
was at grade level. The critical thinking gap ensures that even students
who come to school every single day and do exactly what they are supposed to do will not be prepared for what the future demands.

The critical thinking gap is far from insurmountable because it is a gap
in expectations, not potential. The truth is that students from low-income
backgrounds, students who are linguistically diverse, and students from

minority populations are often endowed with enormous critical thinking potential. Some call this being "street smart," but I reject that categorization. Street smart is just smart. The failure to translate the practical set of problem-solving strategies associated with being street smart to whatever academically amounts to "book smart" is an adult issue, not a child one.

Outside of school, "street smart" children are the young people who are often forced to figure it out. The same ELLs who you might think are uninterested in analyzing nonfiction text at school are helping their families complete complex paperwork in English at home. The same students who did not take the time to analyze the credibility of a source they used in a paper are experts at assessing the credibility of people—a skill they rely on often to navigate their surroundings safely. If our goal is to build a solid house for critical thinking, the foundation and frame is all there. We just need to start building.

It is understandable to feel skeptical about this argument because it sounds a bit idealistic and more than a bit unrealistic. Like, if this idea of "street smart is just smart" is true, then the ramifications would be wild. It would mean that a group of offenders incarcerated in a maximum-security prison for committing violent crimes would theoretically be able to hold their own in a competition against Harvard's debate team who won both national and world debate championships.

But the truth is, in the real-life scenario in 2015 where prisoners formed a debate club while participating in the Bard Prison Initiative—a program where convicts take courses from Bard College—these prisoners did *not* hold their own in a debate against Harvard's team. They *defeated* Harvard, after defeating teams from the United States Military Academy at West Point and from the University of Vermont (CBS News, 2015). Mind you, the inmates did not have access to the internet. The inmates faced delayed access to information for their preparation because the prison administration had to approve any written materials they requested. But in a space where thinking on your toes, playing all the angles, and assessing credibility was valued, "street smart" won the day. In a system where almost 50% of inmates end up back behind bars after release, participants in the Bard Prison Initiative had just a 2% recidivism rate. Lynn Novick, a filmmaker who covered the Bard Prison Initiative for her *College Behind Bars* documentary spoke about these inmates' untapped potential: "Some of the most brilliant students and the greatest intellectual capacity are in places where we don't expect it, and where we have basically, as a society, just said 'We're not going to provide resources because there's nothing there'" (Floyd, 2019).

Our problems are too hard, our needs are too great, and the stakes are just too high to continue to leave brilliance on the table. The "can't, don't, and won't" justifications for allowing the critical thinking gap to go unaddressed are simply untenable. This idea that "kids these days" just cannot think critically ignores the fact that we are responsible for these kids. Instead, "adults these days" need to commit to changing the narrative and stop treating critical thinking as a luxury good. Closing the critical thinking gap for all students is our only hope for giving all students access to 21st-century opportunities. We must overcome the deficit-based practices of focusing on intervention and remediation to the detriment of acceleration and enrichment, a practice that has become even more widespread with school systems' obsession over "learning loss" since the pandemic.

If I had a magic wand, school systems across the country would recognize that leveraging gifted education strategies and instructional practices for the benefit of all students is one of the most tangible ways to close stubborn achievement gaps. An important example of this concept comes from men's college basketball. Opposing teams could not defend against slam dunks by the University of California, Los Angeles's 7'2" center Kareem Abdul-Jabbar (then named Lew Alcindor) and other incredibly gifted athletes, so the National Collegiate Athletics Association decided to ban slam dunks from 1967–1977 (NBC Sports, 2017). Artificially limiting these players' ability in order to make the playing field more competitive is not much different than the common practice of teaching to the middle that ensures high-potential and high-ability students do not get challenged. The slam dunk ban is similar to the underlying motivations of those who advocate in the name of equity for the elimination of gifted and talented programs, magnet schools, and other selective programs.

But less than ten years after the slam dunk ban was repealed in college basketball, the 5'7" Spud Webb (whose hands were not large enough to palm a basketball) defeated his teammate, the 6'8" "Human Highlight Reel" Dominique Wilkins in the National Basketball Association's Slam Dunk Contest. Twenty years later, Spud Webb inspired the 5'9" Nate Robinson to win the Slam Dunk Contest (including a dunk involving Nate Robinson jumping *over* Spud Webb), and Robinson took home first place three times in the next five years! (Manfull, 2006).

I share this anecdote because we often recognize that strategic scaffolds for ELLs and students receiving special educational services help all students. But we less often understand that differentiation for gifted learners has a similar effect. This is why some schools that are looking to increase rigorous learning opportunities for all students require and pay for all of their teachers to receive an endorsement in gifted education. Education equity can't just be about closing achievement gaps. It must be about shattering achievement ceilings. Ensuring that we unleash the full potential of all students, including our gifted and talented students and our highest achievers, is a key strategy for closing the critical thinking gap.

# PART II

## Thinking Like a Lawyer

# Chapter 4

# A Critical Thinking Revolution

When I returned to the classroom in Las Vegas, NV, after teaching in Washington, DC and working in the child welfare system, I was thrilled to get back in the swing of teaching middle and high school math in one of the toughest schools in the city. The Andre Agassi College Preparatory Academy, often called Agassi Prep for short, was a challenging place to work. Friends warned me that I would not have a lot of administrative support, and it was a fair warning. For the first time ever, I saw teachers walk off the job in the middle of the day. Six months into my first year there, teacher turnover was so rapid I could barely remember the names of some of my colleagues as they came and went. Students responded accordingly to this hectic environment. Many of them ended up struggling academically because having a revolving door of teachers each year does not bode well for student achievement. The lack of school structure often impacted student behaviors as well. Even without any of these outside challenges, common issues of poverty also created very real obstacles to learning.

As challenging as teaching at Agassi Prep was, I made it even harder on myself. I made the questionable life decision to go to law school at night as a part-time student at the William S. Boyd School of Law at University of Nevada, Las Vegas. But far from holding me back as a teacher, attending law school ended up becoming the foundation for my transformation

DOI: 10.4324/9781003482147-7

from a "good" teacher to a gap-closing educator. This transformation started with what it meant to be in law school to begin with.

What do you think a law student learns in law school? If you think "the law" is the answer, you are exactly where I was when I applied to law school. But this is not actually true. It turns out that there are too many laws that change all of the time, so it does not make sense for students to sit and memorize different laws. Instead, law school is all about thinking like a lawyer. This concept seemed odd at first, until I started to think about a few of the lawyers I knew.

If you happen to have attorneys as friends, family members, or colleagues, you may know this to be true: lawyers are ridiculously annoying, especially when it comes to answering questions. Say you are having some sort of challenge, like a family law issue, an employment issue, or a friend struggling with an immigration issue. You go to your lawyer friends for some quick advice. (They are lawyers, after all.) This is how they respond:

> "Well, it depends... On one hand... but on the other hand..."
> "I'd need to know more information about..."
> "It could go either way because..."

You immediately regret even asking.

Looking into this trend more deeply, there is likely a reason that 26 past presidents, 35 of our founding fathers, Mahatma Gandhi, and Nelson Mandela have all been attorneys. When people are trained to think like lawyers, they cannot help but approach problems and solutions from multiple angles. As a habit, they ask questions until they get the information they need. It becomes almost instinctual to make different claims and find ways to support these claims with valid and relevant evidence.

As I was realizing what "thinking like a lawyer" meant while teaching middle and high school math at Agassi Prep, I had this revelation: these are the exact same critical thinking skills, habits, and mindsets our students need. Why wait until law school to introduce this powerful framework? This is the same framework used in business school. This is the same method Socrates coined ages ago. There is nothing so special about law school that students should wait until then to get access to this powerful mode of critical thinking.

Let me paint the picture more vividly. As a law student, I took classes on contracts, constitutional law, criminal law, civil procedure, federal income tax, divorce mediation, family law, and wills, trusts, and estates. Across these different contexts, my law school professors asked me to regularly apply a rigorous set of intense inquiry practices. None of this was about rote memorization. In fact, most of my professors allowed students to bring anything ranging from a one-page outline to an entire set of notes and textbooks for final exams.

A decent understanding of the law would get a student a C. Figuring out how to apply the facts in a certain scenario to the law would get a B. The only way to get a coveted A, which is sparsely distributed in law schools, was to be super creative about applying the facts to the law. I had to consider angles that my classmates (who were all on the same mandatory curve) simply did not. I had to make public policy considerations when moving an argument beyond the issue being discussed and weigh the consequences for how this outcome would impact society more broadly.

## Validity and Relevance

Claims matter. Practically speaking, in law school this meant that any time I was faced with a legal issue, my goal was to make a persuasive claim and then determine how to support that claim with evidence that was both valid and relevant. *Valid* means that the evidence used had to be accurate and reliable. *Relevant* means the evidence actually supported the claim. My criminal procedure professor raised my grade by half a point because of my in-class analysis of the *United States v. Drayton* (2002) case about two men convicted of drug trafficking after a police search on a Greyhound bus.[1] Take a look at the facts to see if you notice the same things I did:

> On February 4, 1999, Christopher Drayton and Clifton
> Brown Jr., were traveling on a Greyhound bus en route
> from Ft. Lauderdale, Florida, to Detroit, Michigan.
> The bus made a scheduled stop in Tallahassee, Florida.
> The passengers were required to disembark so the bus
> could be refueled and cleaned... the driver allowed
> three members of the Tallahassee Police Department
> to board the bus as part of a routine drug and weapons

interdiction effort. The officers were dressed in plain clothes and carried concealed weapons and visible badges...

Officer Lang noticed that both respondents [Drayton and Brown] were wearing heavy jackets and baggy pants despite the warm weather. In Lang's experience drug traffickers often use baggy clothing to conceal weapons or narcotics. The officer thus asked Brown if he had any weapons or drugs in his possession. And he asked Brown: "Do you mind if I check your person?" Brown answered, "Sure," and cooperated by leaning up in his seat, pulling a cell phone out of his pocket, and opening up his jacket. Lang reached across Drayton and patted down Brown's jacket and pockets, including his waist area, sides, and upper thighs. In both thigh areas, Lang detected hard objects similar to drug packages detected on other occasions. Lang arrested and hand-cuffed Brown. Officer Hoover escorted Brown from the bus.

Lang then asked Drayton, "Mind if I check you?" Drayton responded by lifting his hands about eight inches from his legs. Lang conducted a pat-down of Drayton's thighs and detected hard objects similar to those found on Brown. He arrested Drayton and escorted him from the bus.

Do you have any doubts about the "facts" of this case? This case is all about whether this was a proper search and seizure under the Fourth Amendment. Do you see what I saw here? Do you believe that the officers' claim that this is a reasonable search process is valid and relevant? I see at least two huge flaws when it comes to the validity here that lead me to doubt whether the officers' actions are justified by accurate or reliable information. The bus originated in Fort Lauderdale and stopped in Tallahassee. But the bus was headed to Detroit in February. Is it really that suspicious to wear large coats when you are headed to Detroit in February? Also, I'm not sure of the officers' reliability because this set of facts seems somewhat questionable. These men were committing a crime. They knew it. Drayton had just seen his partner-in-crime get taken off the bus and arrested because he consented to a voluntary search. How likely does it seem that Drayton would see Brown get arrested and so quickly consent to being searched?

My professor was a former prosecutor and stopped the class at that point to highlight, "This is what analysis looks like. You cannot just look at 'the facts' and blindly accept that these are the facts. You need to understand the story behind the facts." Maybe Officer Lang had had a few arrests overturned because he did not follow the Fourth Amendment guidelines closely enough, so he made sure to create a workable narrative in his police report. Maybe not. In 1999, police reports were not necessarily subject to the same level of skepticism because cell phone videos contradicting police reports did not exist. Since then, police departments across the country have mandated the use of body cameras to improve public trust.

This is not about teaching our students to think of everything they hear as a giant conspiracy theory. It's about ensuring students have a healthy enough sense of skepticism to insist that facts appear to be valid and reliable. Picking apart "facts" is a powerful critical thinking trait that is part and parcel of the thinkLaw framework because it matters for life, academics, and career.

## Considering Multiple Perspectives

As part of the critical thinking process, law school also trains students to consider multiple perspectives of an argument. More precisely, thinking like a lawyer requires students to identify the most significant areas of contention and truly analyze each side of the argument. If we were looking at the dispute between traditional dairy farmers and plant-based producers of products like almond milk and pea milk over what should be called "milk," it is common to lean into your initial bias as you approach the analysis. Farmers tend to lean toward the thinking that "milk has to be milked" and feel that it is fundamentally unfair for companies making a living off of disparaging dairy to still call their products milk.

On the other hand, if it walks like milk and talks like milk, what is the problem with calling it milk? Are traditional dairy farmers going to come after peanut butter companies next because their butter is not really butter? To be clear, the process I'm modeling here is not just about checking off a box that provides some type of argument. Law school expects students to develop persuasive, strong arguments for different perspectives. Even though I did not spend my time as a practicing attorney making my opponents' arguments for them, I did benefit tremendously from preempting their strongest potential arguments.

## Weighing Consequences

Thinking like a lawyer was a powerful framework for critical thinking. The varied nature of the subject matter I learned in law school required these critical thinking tools to be transferred across contexts. But the appeal of this thinkLaw approach goes beyond the benefits for analytical reasoning. There is something galvanizing about an instructional approach grounded in a sense of fairness and justice.

One of the very first cases analyzed in my contracts class was *Lucy v. Zehmer*, a 1954 decision from the Supreme Court of Virginia.[2] The facts were simple: Lucy came into Zehmer's restaurant with a bottle of whiskey, Lucy and Zehmer did lots of drinking, and at some point, they started discussing the selling of Zehmer's farm. On the back of a receipt, Zehmer wrote, "We hereby agree to sell to W.O. Lucy the Ferguson Farm complete for $50,000, title satisfactory to buyer." Lucy took this note to his attorney and sought to enforce this contract, while Zehmer protested that he had been too drunk, and Lucy should have known he was not being serious. The Court enforced the contract, reasoning that whether a contract exists cannot be a question of what a party meant to do. Instead, the Court reasoned, contract formation was about a more objective analysis, looking at actual words and actions.

While students took notes on this case and wrote down the legal rule, I scratched my head. I knew this was the Court's opinion, but I was not okay with this. I get why the Court prefers looking at objective evidence of intent over subjective evidence. But looking at this rule, if I want to score some cheap land, all I need to do is go to my local restaurant, get the owner drunk, and get him to agree to sell land with some scribbles on the back of a napkin? If we analyze the potential consequences of this type of situation, these public policy considerations might lead to a different outcome.

When I realized the patterns of analysis that occurred with almost every legal case we analyzed, thought about, and wrote about in law school—making a claim, making sure the claim was valid and relevant, considering different perspectives, weighing consequences, and drawing a conclusion based on this analysis—I realized how powerful thinking like a lawyer was. When the type of thinking demonstrated in Figure 4.1 is translated to subject areas in K–12 education, it disrupts the system's typical focus on merely finding the "right" answer.

A court's opinion is not a right answer. It is merely a court's opinion. The Supreme Court of the United States in *Plessy v. Ferguson* (1896) had the opinion that "separate, but equal" was just fine.[3] U.S. citizens did not have to accept that. Citizens also did not have to accept the Supreme Court's opinion in *Dred Scott v. Sanford* (1856) that the "negro African race" was "so far inferior, that they had no rights which the white man was bound to respect; and that the negro might justly and lawfully be reduced to slavery for his benefit."[4] When you give students the ability to not just analyze the way the world is, but the critical thinking tools to question the way the world ought to be, students reach a different level of motivation. We have all heard the saying that you can lead a horse to water, but you can't make him drink. When we approach instruction in a way that unleashes our students' inherent sense of justice and fairness (or for teenagers, injustice and unfairness), we're not just leading the horse to water. We are making that horse ridiculously thirsty.

As a lifelong underachiever, I was shocked when I finished my first year of law school with the number one ranking in my class. I had never even been student of the week during my entire K–12 experience! But law school was so fundamentally different than what I was used to. The reason I thrived in law school was the same reason that so many students who were 4.0, high-achievers prior to law school struggled. Law students with a track record of high achievement obsessed with finding the "right"

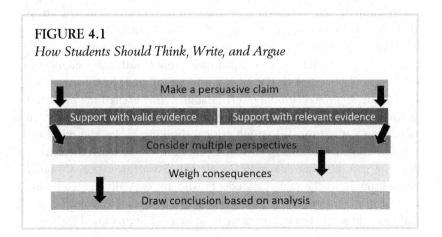

**FIGURE 4.1**
*How Students Should Think, Write, and Argue*

Make a persuasive claim

Support with valid evidence | Support with relevant evidence

Consider multiple perspectives

Weigh consequences

Draw conclusion based on analysis

answer. They spent lots of time memorizing legal rules, but could not think on their toes when asked to apply these rules to the wild concoctions of facts our professors developed for final exams.

Notably, teachers across the country who use the thinkLaw curriculum and use thinkLaw instructional practices report the same counterintuitive findings after introducing this framework to their students. Their high-flying academic students with the best grades struggle with lessons that require them to engage in this type of critical thinking. Meanwhile, struggling learners of all types and "behavior" students stand out like rock stars. After my experience attending law school, this outcome is not surprising to me at all.

Top students are often so conditioned to find the "right" answer that navigating a world that is more gray than black-and-white is challenging. Today's achievers are also achieving in an environment where they learn how to play the game. Show them how to do something, and they'll learn it, memorize, repeat, reuse, and recycle. But developing original thoughts, approaching ideas from nontraditional angles, and navigating problems with a higher degree of nuance are not normally in their toolbox.

Meanwhile, struggling learners end up being uniquely qualified in the 21st-century skill of learning how to learn. Students who hear a teacher explain something and later realize they have no clue what the teacher just said, often end up forcing themselves to make sense of the material on their own. This creativity and resourcefulness gives them a leg up when it comes to wrapping their heads around questions that are more open-ended and leave lots of wiggle room for analysis.

No group of students thinks about alternative theories and unique angles quite like our "behavior" kids can. In fact, I can personally attest to the benefits of spending the bulk of my K–12 experience starting off sentences to my teachers with, "Well, what had happened was…" The same creativity I leaned on to explain away my childhood shenanigans was shockingly similar to the process of finding novel justifications for a defendant to avoid criminal or civil liability. This excited me because I realized that thinkLaw is more than an analytical framework, and even more than a way to instill strong critical thinking habits and mindsets into our students. thinkLaw is also a practical way to close the critical thinking gap. Helping educators to see the powerful critical thinking assets brought to the table by students who are typically denied access because of a fear they are "too low" is an important starting point for creating a world where critical thinking is no longer a luxury good.

thinkLaw also aligns with instructional shifts happening across the country over the past decade in response to a demand for more rigor. As a math teacher who returned to the classroom just in time for the rollout of the Common Core State Standards, I was excited about the overarching instructional practices that guided the math and English language arts college and career readiness guidelines. The thinkLaw framework is inseparable from the first three overarching practices for math:

CCSS.MATH.PRACTICE.MP1. Make sense of problems and persevere in solving them.

CCSS.MATH.PRACTICE.MP2. Reason abstractly and quantitatively.

CCSS.MATH.PRACTICE.MP3. Construct viable arguments and critique the reasoning of others (National Governors Association Center for Best Practices, & Council of Chief State School Officers, 2010).

Thinking like a lawyer also corresponds to all of the Common Core's ELA college and career readiness standards for students:

They demonstrate independence.

They build strong content knowledge.

They respond to the varying demands of audience, task, purpose, and discipline.

They comprehend as well as critique.

They value evidence.

They use technology and digital media strategically and capably.

They come to understand other perspectives and cultures (National Governors Association Center for Best Practices, & Council of Chief State School Officers, 2010).

The entire point of being a lawyer is making sense of problems and sticking with the tricky ones. A lawyer cannot practice law effectively without reasoning in the abstract and the concrete. Almost every billable hour I clocked as an attorney was spent building viable arguments while finding valid ways to shoot down the arguments made by the opposing side. There was no question about the extent to which I needed to "respond to the varying demands of audience, task, purpose, and discipline," "comprehend as well as critique," and "value evidence" as essential parts of thinking like a lawyer.

Even states that never adopted the CCSS, like Texas and Virginia, were still part of a national movement toward more rigorous academic standards. But a lasting challenge of this movement is a lack of understanding of how to move instructional practice to this desired place. If you have children who have started school within the last 8–10 years, you've likely cursed the name of "new math." If you've been in a classroom in the last 8–10 years, you have probably heard the word *rigor* more than you've heard students ask to use the bathroom. And if you've been a school leader in the last 8–10 years, you've probably walked around classrooms and lamented that despite your best coaching efforts, some teachers just don't get it (whatever "it" is) when it comes to rigor. But, as you will soon see, thinkLaw turns the "pie in the sky" concept of rigorous instruction into something far more practical.

Most importantly, thinkLaw flips Bloom's (1956) Taxonomy on its head. I often consider Bloom's Taxonomy to be the most unfortunate diagram in teacher education. The problem is not with the content of the diagram, but with the design of the diagram itself (see Figure 4.2).

The step design, where "remember" and "understand" are at the very bottom and "evaluate" and "create" are at the very top, leads teachers to believe that these levels must always be tackled in order. If this is the case, particularly with students who may be below grade level, it is unsurprising that teachers will not get to critical thinking because students are "too low." This approach ignores the reality that students can evaluate, synthesize, and start the process of higher order thinking before having a full understanding of all of the basics. In fact, a provocative higher order question can often serve as the hook to motivate students to master the lower-level skills needed to answer a question.

Instead, at thinkLaw, we look at a model that simplifies Bloom's taxonomy into four levels of questions and flips the pyramid. With this model, a history teacher can ask eighth graders the Level III evaluative question: "what are the most important factors to consider if you broke up with someone and you were thinking about getting back together with them?" This lesson opener, which I observed in real life, was a powerful hook for a lesson about the Emancipation Proclamation (the breakup) and the Gettysburg Address (the reconciliation attempt). And as you will see demonstrated in the upcoming chapters, this type of low-floor, high-ceiling practice can be used in every grade level and in every subject area.

There is a reason every law school and business school in the United States uses the case method. This type of Socratic-style questioning shifts the power so that teachers are no longer the sage on the stage. Instead, students are the ones who do the heavy lifting in their learning. For gifted

FIGURE 4.2
*Bloom's Taxonomy Diagram*

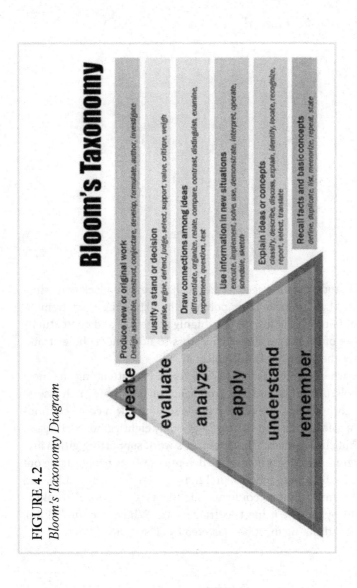

## FIGURE 4.3
*Inverted Questioning Pyramid*

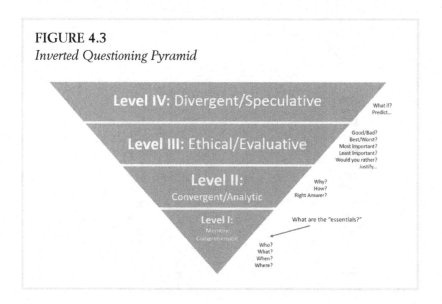

and talented students who need to be pushed beyond black-and-white thinking, thinkLaw unlocks their potential by exploiting their tremendous sense of fairness and justice. The highly accessible and contextually flexible nature of thinkLaw allows educators to implement these strategies no matter the grade level and subject area.

At a time when eighth graders in Las Vegas, NV, attending the most affluent schools, barely cracked 60% proficiency on their state math assessment, and eighth graders attending schools serving low-income communities rarely exceeded the mid-thirties, 74% of my eighth graders at Agassi Prep were proficient. Since then, thinkLaw's work supporting gifted and talented programs, students in juvenile detention, young people aging out of foster care, elite private schools, prekindergarten programs, ELLs, and Title I-funded interventions confirms our theory that critical thinking can be taught by anyone using this framework. Which is quite helpful, because critical thinking must be mastered by all students.

# Notes

1  United States v. Drayton, 536 U.S. 194 (2002).
2  Lucy v. Zehmer, 196 Va. 493, 84 S.E.2d 516 (1954).
3  Plessy v. Ferguson, 163 U.S. 537 (1896).
4  Dred Scott v. Sandford, 60 U.S. 19 (1856).

# Chapter 5

# Introduction to thinkLaw

Thinking like a lawyer extends far beyond anything we would normally consider "the law." From the time you wake up to the time you go to bed, you likely encounter hundreds of moments when critical thinking is required: the warning label about ingesting too much toothpaste, the nutritional facts on your cereal (and the shocking revelation that the amount of cereal poured in your bowl is at least twice the recommended serving size), the terms and conditions you just accepted for that new app that required you to agree to binding arbitration in Antarctica, and even the simple signs you might see on your daily commute. Take this sign for instance:

What does this sign mean? It seems simple enough: no driving in the park. In other words, do you see this park here? Don't drive in it. Very straightforward. You simply cannot drive in the park.

But quick question: can you ride a bicycle in the park? The sign said no driving, so bicycles are probably okay, right? But if the driving restrictions exist for safety reasons, maybe we would not want a bunch of X Games bikers popping wheelies and doing crazy stunts next to the same playground where toddlers play. So maybe we might add in a rule banning the unsafe use of regular bicycles as well. A car certainly won't be allowed, and bicycles have wheels just like cars do. But wait—does that mean I'm now banning wheelchairs from public parks?

DOI: 10.4324/9781003482147-8

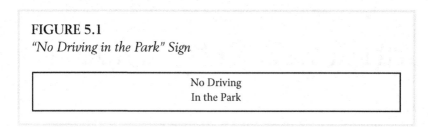

**FIGURE 5.1**
*"No Driving in the Park" Sign*

No Driving
In the Park

What about mopeds? They have a motor, although riding a moped is not quite like driving. But if we allow a moped, next thing you know we'll be allowing motorcycles, and it's a slippery slope. So maybe we should make it clear as to what we mean by *driving*. What if *driving* means directing any moving vehicle that has a motor? Does that work?

Sounds good. But look: that adorable six-year-old happens to have a Jeep Cherokee Power Wheels toy. It has a little motor in there, but it does not exceed three miles per hour. (I might go ahead and ban this out of spite because this is the toy I always wanted as a child that my mother would never get for me.) Some would say that this sort of driving would be okay because it's not *really* driving. So maybe we're now modifying this rule to say that driving is okay only if you aren't in a real car. Do electric cars count? What about driverless ones?

One last thought: we are settling in on this interpretation that you cannot drive in the park with any sort of real motorized vehicle. But suppose a little boy falls off a swing and is bleeding badly. The ambulance comes right away, and the paramedics realize that by cutting through the park and driving up to the boy, they can grab him and get him to the hospital right away. But if they have to walk away from the ambulance, through the park with the stretcher to grab the boy and get him to the hospital, they will lose ten crucial minutes of treatment time. I'm guessing most people would be okay with the ambulance driving through the park to save a boy's life. But we just decided that there was no driving in the park! And more importantly, what if it wasn't an ambulance, but my car, in the same scenario. Would it be okay for me to drive in the park if my son was seriously hurt?

This is a powerful example of the simultaneous approachability and complexity of thinkLaw's practical way of bringing our critical thinking definition to life. Even our youngest learners would have little problem understanding what "No Driving in the Park" means. But thinking about all the potential exceptions and nuances behind this simple meaning exemplifies how educators can use straightforward concepts to build the

crucial critical thinking disposition of inquisitiveness: the habit of probing beyond the surface. And most importantly, it keeps critical thinking
grounded in the notion that Doing Right > Being Right, a notion so crucial
that it's inspired a fashion line of products you can purchase at thinkLaw's
Shopify store online!

Shameless plugs aside, this "No Driving in the Park" exercise has been
a key part of all of thinkLaw's professional learning programs for years
now. But more interestingly, it's been used for our family critical thinking
workshops, where I've learned that a great way to increase attendance at
these things is to ask families to bring their children along. It scares me
to share, however, that in seven years of leading this work, I have never
had a child say it would be okay for me to drive in the park if my son was
seriously hurt. Doing Right > Being Right is not just a cool punchline. It's
a practical remedy for the historical ills of compliance over everything as
the norm. A lot of very bad things have happened in our world's history
because people were just following orders. A lot of very bad things are still
happening today for the same reason. Our ability to thrive as a society
long-term depends on our ability to raise young people who understand
that sometimes driving in the park is what "Doing Right" requires (as long
as they aren't running people over along the way).

# thinkLaw Strategies

The following chapters present five different thinkLaw strategies. Analysis
from Multiple Perspectives is the fundamental thinkLaw strategy that
forms the basis for each of the other strategies. Because of the importance of this framework to the entire thinkLaw methodology, this section
includes one chapter explaining how Analysis from Multiple Perspectives
works and another chapter explaining why it works.

The four other Thinking Like a Lawyer strategies are Mistake Analysis,
Investigation and Discovery, Settlement and Negotiation, and Competition.
For each of these strategies, you will understand the underlying theoreti-
cal framework explaining why and how it works to unleash your students'
critical thinking potential. You will also receive practical examples of how
to connect these strategies to real applications in elementary and secondary classrooms across subject areas. Some of these examples are described
as mini lessons with lots of details. Other examples are simply questions or

short descriptions of how to approach a unit of instruction. For the chapter on Competition, rather than providing subject-specific examples, this chapter will give educators easy-to-implement frameworks they can use to seamlessly integrate Competition into all content areas and grade levels.

These strategies are not designed to be one-size-fits-all solutions. Instead, they are designed to spark a shift in your instruction. As a caution, if you are expecting some sort of massive curriculum overhaul here, you are reading the wrong book. The thinkLaw approach is grounded in the idea that although the critical thinking revolution will not be televised, it has to be practical. With practicality of implementation as the foremost concern, understand that thinkLaw strategies are meant to be curriculum-agnostic tools.

In other words, you can apply these approaches regardless of your school's math and English language arts curriculum or lack thereof. You can seamlessly integrate thinkLaw strategies into a school model that prioritizes project-based learning, STEAM, Montessori, a back-to-basics approach, or dual language programs. In the first edition of this book, examples were limited to the core academic subjects of math, English language arts, social studies, and science. But teachers of the fine arts, physical education, career and technical education, and other elective courses will now find very practical applications and examples for their day-to-day work.

As you read through these thinkLaw frameworks and practical examples of how to apply them, I urge you to think about the ramifications beyond academics. Earlier, we defined critical thinking as having four components:

(1) the set of *skills* and *dispositions* we need
(2) to *learn what we need to learn*
(3) to *solve problems across disciplines*
(4) that are *grounded in the spirit of doing right instead of simply being right.*

ThinkLaw's academic benefits are no more important than the role the framework plays in improving conflict resolution skills, encouraging active citizenship, and building leadership skills. Every educator has a unique role in developing the whole student, so keep an open mind about how you can use thinkLaw strategies to positively shape your students' character, judgment, mindset, and leadership potential.

# Chapter 6

# Analysis from Multiple Perspectives

When it comes to ambivalence, lawyers see multiple sides to it. Fully analyzing any issue requires a careful understanding of all of the different sides to a case. Once this analysis is done, a typical junior attorney at the type of big law firm I worked at must consider several additional questions:

> How will I present this information to the lead partner in this case?
>
> How will I explain this to the client in a way that is likely to under-promise and overdeliver?
>
> How do I structure my arguments to best persuade the grumpy judge reading this brief?
>
> How do I ensure that what I write inflicts maximum damage to the other side's arguments?

Analyzing from multiple perspectives and communicating persuasively to different audiences: this is the foundational thinkLaw strategy. This chapter will present a real-life legal case that illuminates how this works, breaks down precisely why this is such an impactful critical thinking tool, and offers several examples of applying this strategy to instructional practice.

The case Garratt v. Dailey (1955) is a famous personal injury case that most law students study in their first year of law school as part of their

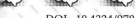  

DOI: 10.4324/9781003482147-9

Torts course.[1] Decided in Washington in 1955, the set of facts in the following section and the court's decision that followed created extremely important precedents in the law. Fortunately for us, it also presents extremely powerful opportunities to develop critical thinking skills and dispositions. When I learned about this case during my first year of my University of Nevada, Las Vegas' law school evening program, I was lucky to have been a classroom teacher by day to see the immediate application of this type of learning experience. Try to think about how your students would react to learning about the case I like to refer to as, "The Chair."

## The Chair

Brian, a five-year-old boy, saw his aunt about to sit down in a chair. Just before his aunt sat down, he pulled out the chair. She fell. She broke her hip. And she suffered $11,000 in medical injuries. She ended up suing Brian for battery. A battery occurs when someone commits (1) an intentional act that (2) involves contact that is (3) harmful or offensive and (4) causes damages. Every single one of these elements will have to be true in order for someone to be liable for battery. Assuming Brian can pay, what is your gut reaction to the following question: *should Brian be liable for battery?*

Most educators would say no, without even thinking about it. This would also be the likely response from a room full of fourth graders, seventh graders, and even twelfth graders. Having asked this question to more than 20,000 educators over the years, I can confidently say that more than 95% of them also share the gut reaction that Brian should not be liable for battery. But challenge yourself to step outside of your initial bias for a second and think about the aunt's argument. How would she argue that Brian should be liable?

Before we analyze the aunt's perspective, there are two important ground rules. First, we cannot make anything up. The entire analysis must be limited to the information given. Second, neither party disputes the facts here. This means that we are taking this entire story to be true on its face. In other words, we know that Brian saw his aunt about to sit. We know that Brian pulled out the chair just before she sat down. We know that she fell and broke her hip. The facts are not in dispute.

Given these facts, the rule for battery, and these ground rules, where should we start? The first step in this type of analysis is narrowing down the core issues. To prove battery, the aunt needs to show that Brian's conduct fulfills all four elements of battery: (1) an intentional act that (2) involves contact that is (3) harmful or offensive and (4) causes damages. Are there any elements here that cannot be reasonably disputed?

Because Brian's aunt broke her hip and had $11,000 in medical expenses, it seems pretty clear that Brian's action of pulling out the chair was harmful and caused her damages. We could claim that his aunt had already broken her hip and fell on purpose so that she could blame it on Brian. But that would involve making up a fact, which violates the ground rules. Also, it seems unlikely that the aunt could have an injury as serious as a broken hip and find a way to play it off long enough to pull off this master scam to get a five-year-old to pay her medical bills. To analyze this case, we really need to focus on whether Brian's act was intentional and whether Brian's act involved contact. Those are the only elements of battery that are seriously in dispute in this case.

Proving intent is tricky, because we cannot look into Brian's head and prove that he pulled out the chair on his aunt on purpose. The goal, then, is to figure out how to explain the facts in such a way that there is no other plausible conclusion a jury can reach but that Brian intentionally pulled out the chair from under his aunt. When we explain these facts, we have to find a simple way to present them. Simplicity matters because juries are full of laypeople who do not know fancy legal mumbo-jumbo and have no desire to learn to speak legalese. What set of facts, simply explained, could lead to a rock-solid conclusion that Brian's act was intentional? Let's look at these facts again:

> Brian, a five-year-old boy, saw his aunt about to sit
> down in a chair. Just before she sat, he pulled out the
> chair. She fell. She broke her hip. And she suffered
> $11,000 in medical injuries.

We know that Brian saw his aunt about to sit down. That seems to support intent, because he clearly knew that she was about to sit. We also know that he physically pulled the chair out. It was not the wind or a second chair-puller. But there is a crucial detail here that often gets overlooked: Brian did not pull out this chair five minutes before, or even five seconds before his aunt sat. He pulled it out "just before she sat." To time this so precisely shows a level of thoughtfulness and calculation that strongly suggests that this was an intentional act.

Piecing this information together in a simple narrative we can present to a jury might sound something like this:

> Your honor, Brian might be five years old. But this particular five-year-old not only saw his aunt about to sit down. He not only pulled out her chair from under her. But he also pulled out the chair from under her at the *exact moment* she was going to sit down. Now, I can't look in Brian's head and prove he did this intentionally. But ladies and gentlemen of the jury... what do *you* think?

This argument sounds compelling, and I know you are likely dying to defend Brian at this point. If you were Brian's attorney, how would you argue against intent? In fact, put yourself in the shoes of a typical sixth grader trying to argue intent. What one key detail would typical sixth graders cling to here that would prevent them from doing any real analysis? If you're thinking Brian's age would be a sticking point, you are correct. I would not be surprised if a sixth grader responded to this question with the three-word essay, "HE IS FIVE!" In other words, five-year-old children likely do not understand the potential consequences of pulling out chairs. This is probably true, because most five-year-old children do not purposely try to hospitalize their relatives. But if your best argument is "Brian is too young" or "Brian meant it as a joke," that probably is not good enough. You cannot go to court arguing that a woman's broken hip was just a joke that went bad.

Let's look at these facts again:

> Brian, a five-year-old boy, saw his aunt about to sit down in a chair. Just before she sat, he pulled out the chair. She fell. She broke her hip. And she suffered $11,000 in medical injuries.

Is there a way we can look at this same exact set of facts, but tell a different story? We know that Brian saw his aunt about to sit and pulled out the chair right before she sat. But we don't know why he did this. What if he was trying to help her? If Brian was a gentleman-in-training, then it would make perfect sense that he would see her about sit and pull out the chair just before she sat. And why did she fall? Because he is five years old, and children do not have the best hand-eye coordination, fine motor skills, or depth perception. Or maybe he just left out the crucial step of scooting the chair in a bit as she was going to sit down. In any case, I am not sure how much I buy this argument. But if this accident occurred under this gentleman-in-training theory, then by definition it cannot be intentional.

Moving on to the contact element, what makes proving contact tricky? There was no direct touching here. Brian pulled the chair, and his aunt's behind hit the floor. But the aunt's attorney must find some way around the fact that there was no direct contact. Brian saw her about to sit. It might be helpful to consider whether eye contact is enough to meet the contact requirement. But what would the world look like if giving someone the stink-eye was enough to be liable for a battery? That argument is probably not the best idea.

We do know that Brian made contact with the chair in such a way that it caused his aunt to make contact with the floor. Can we make an argument that says that the chair bone is connected to the butt bone, which is connected to the floor bone? This idea that the chair and floor become an extension of the aunt's body under these circumstances is helpful, but still a little confusing for laypersons sitting on a jury.

If I am the aunt's attorney, I probably want to help the jury understand the public policy implications of what happens if Brian's action is not considered to be a contact. What would the world look like if a battery could only occur with direct contact? A person could run over someone with a car and say, "Technically, your honor, the bumper hit him." And the judge would say, "Okay, no direct touching, case closed." Complete defenses to battery claims would include "the knife stabbed him," "the bullet hurt him," or "the brick hit him in the head." So maybe there is a continuum here, where on one end, there is direct contact, like punching someone in the face, and on the other end, we can blame the bartender.

What bartender? Well, it turns out that on the night Brian was conceived, his mother and father were enjoying margaritas, and the bartender was being extra generous with his tequila pours. Five years and ten months later, Brian broke his aunt's hip. If the bartender never got the party started, Brian would have never been conceived and would not have had the opportunity to pull out the chair on his aunt. This bartender theory obviously goes way too far to prove causation. There are limits, therefore, to the "but-for" type of reasoning you can apply here. But on that same "but-for" continuum, pulling out a chair on someone just before they sit is probably a lot closer to the type of act that should be considered a contact.

A lot of educators define critical thinking as "analysis with an absence of emotion." In other words, they would say critical thinking is about rational thinking, while thinking based on your emotions, on the other hand, is inherently irrational. I view the relationship between critical thinking and emotions with a bit more nuance. To understand why, take a look at where your thinking is right now. After analyzing intent and contact, I want you to go back to your original reading of these facts:

> Brian, a five-year-old boy, saw his aunt about to sit down in a chair. Just before she sat, he pulled out the chair. She fell. She broke her hip. And she suffered $11,000 in medical injuries.

Compared to the first time you read these facts, do you now think this case might be more complicated or more nuanced than you originally thought? Think of this as an example of developing your critical thinking dispositions—specifically, the habit of looking beyond the surface. You read this emotionally shocking set of facts that sparked an immediate reaction. You made a gut judgment without fully analyzing all of the details. But you have a mature enough critical thinking disposition to understand that your gut reaction is based on emotion. And you understand that your gut feeling is not yet supported by any real analysis.

Imagine if all students had this healthy sense of skepticism, causing them to look deeper into information that seems simple on its surface. Imagine if adults did this on social media. Before ranting and raving about an article after reading the headline, what if adults actually read the article first? The simple act of stepping outside of your initial bias and arguing for the aunt in a case that seems silly on its surface forces a much more nuanced analysis. This type of thinking process repeated over time develops the transferable critical thinking skills and mindsets our students need.

Looking beyond the facts, it is helpful to take a step back and ask about the elephant in the room. What seems weird about this case? It seems weird for an aunt to sue her own nephew, especially because he is only five years old. With that said, what is the real story here? What are the behind-the-scenes details that might be motivating this lawsuit? Your wheels are probably spinning right now. Maybe you are thinking about family drama, specifically the idea that the aunt may have some issues with Brian's parents. Maybe you see this as an insurance issue; maybe the aunt was somehow required to sue Brian to trigger insurance coverage because she really needed the money. Speaking of money, maybe Brian is sitting on a nice trust fund, and his side of the family is loaded. This is the right house to get injured at! Or maybe there is a corrective motivation here because Brian could be a complete rascal who has done things like this hundreds of times with no accountability.

Your specific theory of the case does not matter. What does matter is that if this was history class and you asked students who was the most influential figure of the progressive era, or if this was science and you asked students to predict what was causing a chemical reaction to occur, too often the default response is "I don't know" or the infamous blank stare. But when you tap into your students' inherent sense of justice and fairness, it's like they'll go to the edge of the earth for Brian. They look beyond the page, seamlessly making predictions and inferences.

We can even extend this to big picture, public policy questions. What would the world look like if children could just go around pulling out chairs on people who get seriously hurt, but those victims could not recover because the aggressors were too young? At the same time, what would the world look like if adults could just go around suing five-year-old children every time the kids made a practical joke that went wrong? Neither world is ideal, but which world would you prefer to live in?

At this point, we have taken a concept that is so conceptually simple it can be introduced in elementary school, but we have extended the level of rigor to what could be seen in any law school or courtroom. The best part is that students do not even know what is going on here. They have no clue they are engaged in a standards-aligned critical thinking activity at the highest levels of Bloom's (1956) Taxonomy, Webb's (1999) Depth of Knowledge, or whatever rigor standard you are most familiar with. Students are just enjoying the fight for Brian's rights! And for teachers who make big picture questions like this the climax of their instruction, this becomes a practical tool to shift the power. Big picture questions help teachers transition from being the sage on the stage to facilitators who galvanize students to do the heavy lifting in their own learning.

# The "Answer"

With all of this in mind, have you changed your opinion? After analyzing the aunt's case in more detail, has your decision about holding Brian liable for battery changed? Whether it did or it didn't, is there a difference between what *you* think the outcome should be versus what *a judge* might decide? Often, thinkers who do not believe Brian should be liable think that a judge would find Brian liable. They reason that a judge is more objective and will look at just the facts, while they are less rational, thinking more about issues that go beyond the facts. However, there is a simpler explanation for this tension that makes sense once we look at the court's decision.

The court decided that Brian was liable for battery. The court reasoned that although Brian probably did not intend to break his aunt's hip, the intent to cause harm was not the issue. The only intent that mattered was Brian's intent to pull out the chair. Although there was no direct contact, it was substantially certain that contact would result from pulling out a chair from under someone at the same exact moment that person is about to sit. Some of you reading this will not like this decision.

And that is fine. This is not a right answer. This is merely a court's decision. A court once upheld a law banning interracial marriage, reasoning that both races were not allowed to marry each other, so it was fair! A court gave the thumbs-up to Japanese internment camps. Other courts decided that neither Japanese nor Indian nationals could be eligible to become United States citizens. But citizens did not have to accept these decisions as the final answer. In other words, the tension that you may be struggling with after reading the outcome in Brian's case is a good tension. It is one thing to give our students critical thinking tools to analyze the world the way it is. It is significantly more powerful to give them the tools to question the way the world ought to be.

Analysis From Multiple Perspectives is the foundation of the thinkLaw approach because of cases like this one. Advocating for someone's position when we do not necessarily care for that someone is challenging. Analyzing why we might want to hold someone accountable when we feel extremely sympathetic toward them and fundamentally do not want to hold them accountable is challenging. But these are good challenges—challenges grounded in productive struggle that force us to not only analyze deeply, but also shift our habits of thinking about problems like these.

And when you add in the additional layer of needing to articulate a persuasive argument to a wide variety of audiences, educators emphasizing analysis from multiple perspectives have now made enormous strides in building up learners who can listen to understand, speak to be understood, and disagree without being disagreeable, a topic discussed more in Chapter 12 of this book.

# Note

1  Garratt v. Dailey, 46 Wash. 2d 197 (Wash., 1955).

# Chapter 7

# The Power of Analysis from Multiple Perspectives

In the last chapter, I used over 3,000 words to analyze three lines of text written at a second grade level. There are three reasons the thinkLaw strategy of Analysis from Multiple Perspectives has such powerful implications for critical thinking in the classroom:

1. Multiple perspective analysis unlocks students' motivation and agency.
2. It provides a practical tool to build empathy at a time when social-emotional learning (SEL) is more important than ever.
3. Most importantly, multiple perspective analysis is the foundation of thinkLaw's framework for critical thinking across grade levels and subject areas.

This chapter will take a deeper look at these three implications.

## Motivation and Agency

When you imagine leading an activity like "The Chair" (see p. X) in a classroom, you can probably feel the energy. During learning moments

DOI: 10.4324/9781003482147-10

like this, no student yells out, "Is this going to be on the test?" No one asks, "Are we getting graded for this?" There is a different level of buy-in that goes beyond engagement. The term *student engagement* is thrown around so often that teachers sometimes forget that engaged students are not necessarily learning. But when that engagement is purposefully designed to unlock students' inherent motivation and agency, this is a key factor in building the desire to learn deeply.

What does motivation and agency look like? When learning about "The Chair," students are not in the experience for the gold star or the check mark; it's deeper than that. A five-year-old child's future is at stake! This intrinsic drive is often associated with justice and fairness, conflict, drama, investigations, and competition.

There is also something powerful about students being able to build relationships as part of a meaningful and autonomous learning experience. To get to this point, students must feel competent to successfully achieve the learning goals. In "The Chair" example, learners do not need to go to law school to thoughtfully engage in the learning process as they analyze the case. Because of this confidence, students working in groups build on each other's ideas, push each other's creativity, and laugh as they pontificate.

This leads me to an important note about grit. What would be your response to the following true-or-false statement: "students really don't have grit, and if they had grit, they would be a lot more successful?" Years ago, I would have said this was true without hesitation. But after having opportunities to interact with young people across the country inside and outside of the formal education system, I am certain that educators do not truly understand grit.

I know young people living in border communities in Texas and Arizona who travel up to two and a half hours each day to go to school because they return to Mexico every night. I know young people who navigate dangerous neighborhoods and challenging family situations every single day to make it to school. I also know many young people who have no issue pulling an all-nighter to solve highly complex problems. Granted, these complex problems tend to be in the form of whatever the latest gaming craze is. But each of these cases shows that the issue is not that students do not have grit. In so many ways, seen and unseen, our students have more grit than we could ever imagine. Our challenge as educators is: how do we create frequent opportunities for students to exercise their grittiness?

Agency is a helpful counter-narrative for the misguided idea of grit. It is common to heared the phrase "empowering students" as a desired outcome of student-centered learning. But as I discuss in my second book, *Tangible Equity: A Guide for Leveraging Student Identity, Culture, and Power to Unlock Excellence In and Beyond the Classroom*, "empowerment" misses the point (Seale, 2022). When educators create classroom experiences grounded in critical thinking that unlock student motivation, we are helping students recognize the power they already possess.

## Building Empathy

At first glance, it feels wrong for an aunt to sue her own five-year-old nephew. But when we start looking into the aunt's side and walk in her shoes, her situation seems pretty awful as well—she has all of these medical bills and is struggling with a broken hip. What if this aunt were your mother? What if this aunt was you?

The simple exercise of developing a plausible argument for a side you do not agree with is a powerful tool. The ability to put oneself in the shoes of others to experience a conflict from their point of view is the essence of empathy. With social-emotional learning becoming thing number 89 million on educators' responsibility list, it is a relief that we do not have to choose between rigorous academic content and SEL. Analysis from multiple perspectives accomplishes both goals simultaneously.

## The thinkLaw Framework: DRAAW+C

There seems to be no shortage of viral crazes that exploit the gung-ho nature of how the masses tend to approach decisions. Watch any news or sports network and you will similarly see panels where the speakers do nothing but rattle off the points for their side. Fortunately, thinkLaw's model for Analysis from Multiple Perspectives creates a concrete framework for moving toward a much more thoughtful reasoning process.

A universal framework for critical thinking across grade levels and subject areas—and even for leadership, parenting, and decision making in general—might look something like Figure 7.1. When making an argument, students should make sure that any claim they attempt to make is supported by evidence. This evidence must be valid: reliable, trustworthy, and up to date. It must also be relevant, which requires the evidence to actually support the claim they are attempting to make.

As a part of this process, students should consider multiple perspectives. They will want to serve as a true devil's advocate for the opposing claim to help guide their thinking. Then, they should make sure they think about the consequences of their decision. Asking "what would the world look like if…" helps students to see beyond the issue right in front of them and visualize the potential impact. How might their decision alter a long-standing rule or norm? Is this one of the issues where the consequences of being right are less important than doing right?

Finally, students' conclusions should flow directly from this analysis. Often, students approach this the other way; they know the conclusion they want, so they move heaven and earth to reach this conclusion. They cite dubious sources that they know are not valid or bring in random evidence that has nothing to do with the claim in question. They stack the deck with nothing but information that supports their side. The only consequence they care about is the consequence of not reaching their desired outcome.

thinkLaw has simplified this process with a framework called DRAAW+C (see Figure 7.2). This structure is easy to follow whenever students have a decision or assignment that requires critical thinking. They start with a decision: *Who should win? What is the best course of action?*

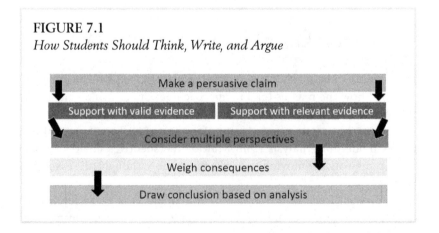

FIGURE 7.1
*How Students Should Think, Write, and Argue*

---

**FIGURE 7.2**
*DRAAW+C Framework*

**D**ecision: Who should win?

**R**ule/Law: What is the rule or law for this case?

**A**rguments Plantiff will make: All evidence, facts, and arguments the person bringing the lawsuit will use.

**A**rguments Defendant will make: All evidence, facts, and arguments the person defending the lawsuit will use.

**W**orld: Looking at the big picture, why is your decision better for the world than the other possible decisions?

**C**onclusion: Rewrite the decision as a conclusion.

---

*Which person will you select?* Then they restate the rule, law, property of math, rule of grammar, theory of science, or another logical basis for their claim.

If students are explaining who they think the most influential figure of the Progressive Era is, they might explain the rule like this: "To be the most influential figure of the Progressive Era, the person's actions must be directly responsible for impacting the most change on the United States between the 1890s and 1920s." If students are taking a course on Western art history and classifying what period of art a picture is from, they might decide a piece is Neoclassical and use a rule that says, "In Neoclassical art, the painted subjects look like they can be statues with very clear and sharp outlines."

Then, students get to their arguments. At a minimum, they want to provide a strong argument and counterargument, but many issues are not simple matters of "on one hand... but on the other hand." As discussed in Chapter 10: Settlement and Negotiation, students might need to analyze three or more competing arguments. Additionally, as a teacher, you can be flexible on your requirements for this piece. If you work in elementary grades, you might want students to simply write one sentence for the argument and one sentence for the counterargument. This might extend to entire paragraphs in secondary grades, making multiple points for each argument and counterargument.

The "World" component of DRAAW+C transforms a good argument into a powerful one. The sample DRAAW+C response in Figure 7.3 is from a third grade student. He is already on his way when he hits his arguments and counterarguments: "The aunt will argue that Brian moved the chair on purpose and knew that she would fall. Brian will argue that he is only five. He didn't know that she would get hurt." But the student takes this response to another level with his analysis of how a decision against

FIGURE 7.3
*Third Grade Student's DRAAW+C Response*

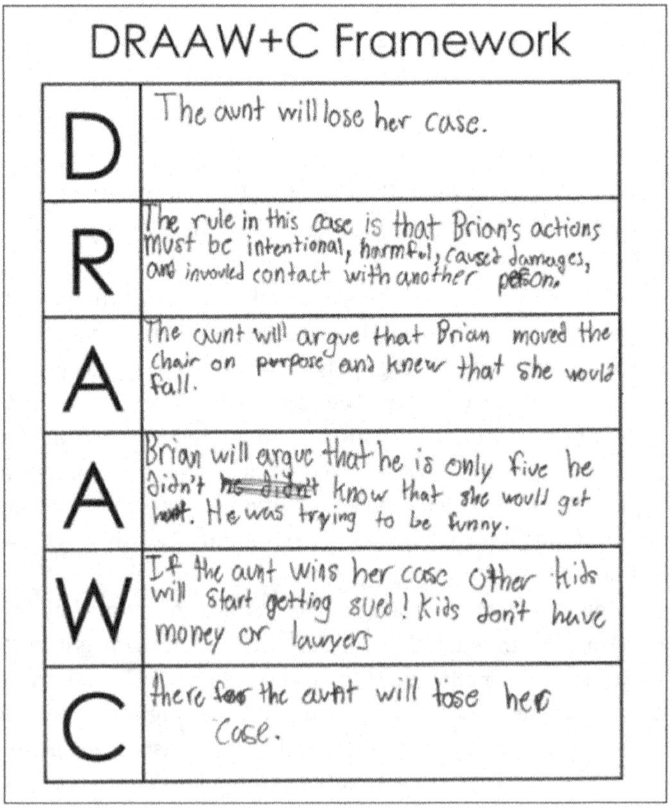

| DRAAW+C Framework | |
|---|---|
| **D** | The aunt will lose her case. |
| **R** | The rule in this case is that Brion's actions must be intentional, harmful, caused damages, and involved contact with another person. |
| **A** | The aunt will argue that Brian moved the chair on purpose and knew that she would fall. |
| **A** | Brian will argue that he is only five he didn't ~~he didn't~~ know that she would get hurt. He was trying to be funny. |
| **W** | If the aunt wins her case other kids will start getting sued! Kids don't have money or lawyers |
| **C** | there for the aunt will lose her case. |

Brian would negatively impact public policy in future cases like this one: "If the aunt wins her case, other kids will start getting sued. Kids don't have money or lawyers!"

The reasoning for the "World" component might sound familiar because it is one of the most common kinds of responses: the "opening the floodgates" argument. An example might look like this: "If you let a woman win a lawsuit because her coffee was too hot, it will open the floodgates for all sorts of crazy cases. Next thing you know, someone will sue an iron manufacturer because he was burned by the iron when he ironed his clothes while wearing them!" This response is in the same family as the "slippery slope" argument: "If you legalize medical marijuana, it will lead to a slippery slope that ends in the complete legalization of all drugs." Although taken to the extreme, "slippery slope" arguments are logical fallacies, the main idea is to help thinkers start to see beyond the issue at hand and analyze the precedential value of a decision. The key component of any effective "World" response is a clear explanation of why the world would be better (or worse) because of a decision.

Finally, the conclusion, like any solid conclusion, restates the key arguments without raising any new points. Figure 7.4 is a rubric that demonstrates how DRAAW+C can be evaluated.

# Examples of Analysis from Multiple Perspectives

## *Who Should Win?*

Who Should Win? is the basic set up for any learning experience designed for students to analyze problems from multiple perspectives. Here are the steps to setting this up:

1. Pick the question stem: who, what.
2. Pick what type of ranking you want to perform: best/worst, most influential/least important, overrated/underrated, shadiest, most annoying, fastest way to solve/slowest way to solve, easiest way to solve/hardest way to solve, most reliable/least reliable.

## FIGURE 7.4
*DRAAW+C Rubric*

| | 3 Points | 2 Points | 1 Point |
|---|---|---|---|
| Decision | Clearly states a claim about who should win the case. | States a vague claim that does not clearly identify who the winner should be. | Does not make a claim about who should win the case. |
| Rule/Law | Clearly explains what rule or law applies to the case, predicting or synthesizing the legal rule if necessary. | Identifies a rule or law that should apply to the case but does not clearly explain what that rule or law is. | Does not identify a rule that should apply to the case. |
| Arguments for the Plaintiff | Clearly identifies the most persuasive evidence, facts, and arguments the person bringing the lawsuit should use. | Identifies evidence, facts, and arguments for the person bringing the lawsuit but does not include all of the most relevant evidence, facts, and arguments. | Omits all or almost all evidence, facts, and arguments for the person bringing the lawsuit. |
| Arguments for the Defendant | Clearly identifies the most persuasive evidence, facts, and arguments the person defending the lawsuit should use. | Identifies evidence, facts, and arguments for the person defending the lawsuit but does not include all of the most relevant evidence, facts, and arguments. | Omits all or almost all evidence, facts, and arguments for the person defending the lawsuit. |
| World | Clearly explains why public policy (the world) will be better off if the decision is reached. | Address public policy but does not clearly explain why the world will be better off if the decision is reached. | Omits all or almost all arguments addressing public policy. |
| Conclusion | Clearly states a conclusion that summarizes the key arguments without raising new points not discussed in the preceding sections. | Concludes without summarizing key arguments or raises new points not discussed in the preceding sections. | Omits a conclusion. |

3. Pick what you want to rank: character, historical figure, scientific procedure, sentence, essay, artist, musician.
4. Require justification: why? (Students should use the DRAAW+C framework for this analysis.)

# *Example:*

**D:** Goldilocks is the shadiest fairy tale character of all time.

**R:** A person is shady if she is of doubtful honesty or legality.

**A:** In "Goldilocks and the Three Bears," not only did Goldilocks commit the crime of breaking and entering into someone's home, but she also violated the bears' space in so many ways. She sat all up in their chairs, breaking the little bear's chair. She put her germs all up in other people's porridge she decided to eat without permission, eating all of little bear's porridge. And then she had the audacity to get in all of their beds—again, sticking it to little bear by sleeping in his bed.

**A:** Goldilocks might argue that she was just a lost and hungry girl in the forest seeking shelter and food. She might use this innocence to place the title of shadiest fairy tale character on the Big Bad Wolf, who wreaked havoc with both "Little Red Riding Hood" and "The Three Little Pigs."

**W:** If people like Goldilocks were able to get away with ransacking the homes of strangers because they were lost, it would encourage children who are lost to just break into homes instead of asking for help, putting children in danger.

**C:** Therefore, because of the brazen nature of Goldilocks's actions and the harmful impact conduct like this would have on keeping children safe, Goldilocks is the shadiest fairy tale character ever.

## Examples of Who Should Win? Across Content Areas

**Math:** What is the best way to solve a system of equations? Why? We just completed a unit on adding, subtracting, multiplying, and dividing fractions. Rank these operations from the easiest to the hardest and explain your rankings. Between the radius, diameter, and circumference, what is the most important component of a circle?

**English and Language Arts:** Rank the main characters of this novel from worst to best and explain your rankings. Out of the three main pieces of information in this nonfiction passage, which one was the most significant? The Three Bears are writing a letter to the Court asking Goldilocks to repair the damages she caused in their home. Goldilocks will have to write her own letter defending her actions, explaining why she should not be required to repair these. Write both letters based on the same set of facts.

**Foreign Language:** How can you communicate a phrase logically in your foreign language using the fewest number of words? Using the maximum number of words? For any given topic, is it harder to comprehend reading, speaking, or listening to the foreign language example? Why?

**Social Studies:** Who was the most influential African American inventor, and why? Was Alexander the Great really all that great? What would various stakeholder groups have to say about that? What was the most significant event in the lead up to ___? Explain. If we had to get rid of one branch of federal government, which one would it be and why?

**Science:** What are the strongest arguments you could use to convince a "Flat Earther" that the Earth is round? What is the most important cell organelle/body organ/body system and why? What is the most important property of an element? What one step can be removed from the scientific method to have the least harm on the results of the experiment?

**Career and Technical Education:** There are three different ways to do a certain task (in cooking, welding, early childhood care, etc.). Which one do you prefer and why? In a marketing class, students are completing a marketing plan for a new pizza spot with a limited marketing budget. Rank the top three social media platforms they should consider advertising on and explain your rankings.

**Physical Education:** In the five minutes it takes to explain to students the rules of a new game or activity, ask students to explain what is the most important rule to remember and why. For example, if students are playing dodgeball, there is a case as to whether no aiming for the face could be a more important rule than the honor code of gracefully bowing out of the game when you get hit (which might lead to you getting hit in the face). When students have to select teams of mixed abilities, what is the most important factor (other than skill, talent, strength, etc.) to consider in selecting a "good" teammate?

**Fine Arts:** When deciding the genre/time period/era for a piece of art or a piece of music, what are the best arguments for the work to be classified as another genre/time period/era? What is the most memorable/important part of a work of art? What emoji best describes the emotional reaction to a work of art? In theater, what character do you personally relate to the most and why? If you are playing a character yourself, what aspect of that person's character do you have the most trouble connecting with and why?

# Chapter 8

# Mistake Analysis

Everything written in this book so far about increasing access to critical thinking in the classroom only makes sense if students have the psychological safety to think critically. In my work with schools across the country, I have asked teachers to collect student responses to a survey thinkLaw developed to measure critical thinking dispositions. Based on responses from thousands of students, 68% at least "somewhat agreed" that they do not like sharing answers in class if they are not sure they are correct (see Figure 8.1). With perfectionism being such a rampant challenge for gifted and high-achieving students in particular, this fear of making mistakes has powerful ramifications.

I recently met a woman who served as a student advisor at a university's engineering college. Her school is ranked in the top 75 of all engineering colleges, and she let me in on a surprising secret: a council of employers closely connected to the university explicitly asked her and her team to "stop sending 4.0 students." These employers complained that these academic high achievers had no capacity to deal with failure in an industry that is fundamentally based on failure. Instead, the employers were asking for students who could navigate imperfection, manage the struggle, and understand that mistakes are opportunities for learning.

Mistakes are the essence of a lawyer's universe. Understanding mistakes, mitigating mistakes, and arguing that one side's mistakes are less

DOI: 10.4324/9781003482147-11

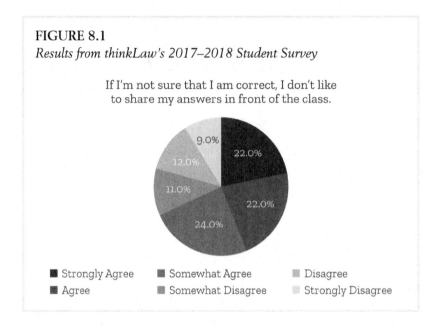

**FIGURE 8.1**
*Results from thinkLaw's 2017–2018 Student Survey*

If I'm not sure that I am correct, I don't like
to share my answers in front of the class.

9.0%
22.0%
12.0%
11.0%
22.0%
24.0%

■ Strongly Agree     ■ Somewhat Agree     ▨ Disagree
■ Agree              ■ Somewhat Disagree  ▨ Strongly Disagree

severe than the other side's mistakes are part of the day-to-day experience of practicing law. And it turns out that mistake analysis is also a very
practical, but powerful way to increase psychological safety for students
in the classroom.

# The Golf Club

Here's an example of how Mistake Analysis appears in the world. Consider
the following real-life case (Lubitz v. Wells, 1955):

> James (11 years old) was playing with Judith (9 years
> old) in James's backyard when he saw a golf club that
> his father, Mr. Wells, left outside. James picked up the
> golf club and swung it at a rock lying on the ground.
> While James swung the golf club, he hit Judith's jaw and
> chin with the golf club, shattering Judith's jaw. Judith
> sued James's father, Mr. Wells.[1]

# Two Questions to Explore Are

1. What mistake do we need to focus on here?
2. What is the most important question we need to ask about this mistake?

At first glance, it might seem like the mistake we care about most is James hitting Judith in her jaw. This is what has caused the most damage, after all. However, Judith is suing Mr. Wells, not his son. Mr. Wells didn't do anything. The mistake we really care about analyzing, therefore, is this act of inaction: Mr. Wells leaving the golf club outside in the backyard.

Moving on to the second question is tricky. Yes, it would be somewhat helpful to know why Mr. Wells left the golf club out. But whatever thinking or lack of thinking motivated his decision to leave the golf club outside is likely less important than the fact that it was left out to begin with.

As we think about this injury, tragic as it is, we will probably start thinking about the object itself. It is a golf club, not a gun or a samurai sword. What's the difference between a golf club and a samurai sword? Swords are designed to be dangerous; golf clubs are not. The most important question to ask, therefore, might be, "Is a golf club an inherently dangerous object?" Or, if we are acting as Judith's attorney, we might ask whether a golf club is an inherently dangerous object in the hands of an 11-year-old child like James. If James himself is a particularly mischievous child, Mr. Wells might have reason to know that even a pencil could be a dangerous object in James' hands! In either case, focusing on this mistake is a very different sort of analysis than most students are used to. The "wrong" has already happened, so there's no reason to fear making a mistake. This is why Mistake Analysis is so powerful as a thinkLaw strategy.

There are two specific thinkLaw strategies you can use to lean into mistakes as critical thinking opportunities: (1) Which Wrong Is More Right? and (2) What Would Joe Schmo Do?

# Which Wrong Is More Right?

Solve this equation: $2x + 8 = 20$

This is a basic, skills-based question that would simply assess whether a student can perform the routine procedure of solving a two-step equation.

If you wanted to increase the rigor for a problem like this in your classroom, you might ask the question like this:

Colin tried to solve this problem. What did he do wrong?

$2x + 8 = 20$

$2x = 10$

$x = 5$

If you wanted to use Mistake Analysis as a way to apply the DRAAW+C critical thinking framework, ask students to look at a minimum of two incorrect answers to ask which one is more "right." In this math problem example, a classroom could be divided into two groups, each one representing one of the sides in Figure 8.2. One group would serve as the lawyers for the left-hand side, and the other group would represent the right-hand side. The strategy for solving this problem is twofold. First, students would need to develop the most innocent interpretation of their side's mistake. Then, they would need to think about the most moronic interpretation of the other side's mistake.

A student representing the left-hand side might look at the mistake and call it a tiny subtraction error. "20 – 8" should be 12, but 10 is close enough. Besides, x = 5 is only 1 away from the correct answer of x = 6. If we started the process of checking the work by going backward, plugging in x = 5 to the equation 2x = 10 would give the right answer. On the other hand, on the right-hand side, the solver performed the first step correctly but did not understand that a two-step equation has two different steps.

FIGURE 8.2

*Which One Is More Right?*

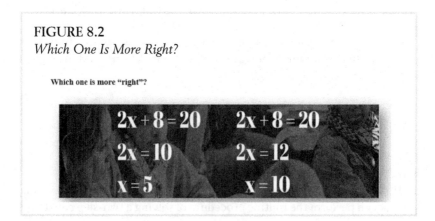

Which one is more "right"?

The solver clearly does not understand that 2x is a multiplication expression that requires the inverse operation of division.

The right-hand side is far from defenseless, however. A student representing the right-hand side can pick apart the left-hand side's claims that their solver only made a small subtraction error. This is not just any subtraction error; it is an error in the very first step of the problem. If a person is already messing up in the first step of a problem, they're hopeless! Also, this might not even be a simple subtraction error. The solver could have instead made the shocking error of combining 2x and 8 to get a 10 and just bringing the 2x down to the next step of the problem. If the student defending the right-hand side wants to get really creative, they might argue that every single line of their problem is actually true. Subtracting 8 from both sides of the equation correctly results in the equation $2x = 12$. It is also true that $x = 10$ (at least, if x is the Roman numeral $X$).

Stop and think for a second about what cognitive skills students employ to conduct this analysis. They are no longer asking "what" and "how to." They are now in the world of "why" and "what if." They are going beyond metacognition, where they think about their own thinking processes. They are now analyzing the hypothetical thinking patterns of others and evaluating those patterns against each other.

Note that this is not the same as the exercise of looking at an incorrect answer and asking, "what did this student do wrong?" Correcting someone's mistake is an example of a question that truly has just one correct answer. Mistake Analysis with critical thinking requires the extra step of some level of comparative analysis and ranking.

Using Mistake Analysis as part of the DRAAW+C framework, a student's response might look something like this:

> **D:** The left-hand side is more "right."
>
> **R:** To solve a two-step equation, you have to isolate the variable by applying the correct inverse operations to eliminate all constants and coefficients until the only thing left is the variable on one side and a value on the other.
>
> **A:** The left-hand side made a small subtraction error in the first step but completed the problem correctly after that step. That side's final answer was also closer to the actual correct answer.

**A:** The right-hand side subtracted correctly in the first step but subtracted in the second step when division was required. But both of the operations were performed correctly.

**W:** If the right-hand side received more points than the left-hand side, we would be living in a world where computational accuracy was more important than conceptual understanding. Who cares if you subtract correctly when you're actually supposed to be dividing? If you ran a bank, it would be a much smaller error to make a subtraction mistake when you're supposed to be subtracting than to correctly subtract when you're supposed to be dividing.

**C:** Therefore, the left-hand side should get more credit for this problem.

Using Mistake Analysis here is a powerful way to exploit the drama and conflict that so often taps into our students' motivation and agency. Students who "don't do math" still do drama and conflict. Additionally, this creates real opportunities for meaningful writing experiences in math. So often, writing in math is limited to explaining how to solve a problem. Incorporating DRAAW+C into Mistake Analysis results in a much more thoughtful, organized form of persuasive writing that is transferable across all subject areas.

## What Would Joe Schmo Do?

Another way to change attitudes and mindsets toward mistakes while incorporating critical thinking is to focus on Joe Schmo. Joe Schmo is a fictional person I created in my classroom who we all have some familiarity with. Joe always falls for the trick answer. Joe does not read the directions carefully. Joe does not complete all of the steps in a problem. We all know Joe Schmo, and I can prove it.

Suppose I am looking at a very cool "Don't Raise Your Voice. Improve Your Argument." t-shirt from the thinkLaw Shopify site that costs $30 and notice that today it is on sale for 10% off. What is the final price of this shirt? Rather than solving for the final price, imagine that we are playing *Family Feud* and we have surveyed 100 Joe Schmos to find out what the final price is of a t-shirt that costs $30 and is on sale for 10%. What would be the number one Joe Schmo answer? If you are channeling your inner Joe Schmo correctly, 20 would be your answer. Joe Schmo is most likely to see $30, see the 10%, ignore the percentage sign, and just subtract 10 from 30. If this is a multiple-choice test, you can bet good money that 20 will be a potential response.

Let's take it one step further. What two other Joe Schmo answers to the question might make the *Family Feud* board? The t-shirt costs $30 and is on sale for 10% off. Joe Schmo could certainly select $3 as his answer. Joe Schmo might know something about percent problems. He multiplies $30 by .10, and he sees that 3 is the answer. He looks at the answer choices, and, of course, $3 is an option. So, he's done! He might make a different mistake, realizing he has to take 10% off of $30. So, he turns 10% into .10, subtracts that from $30, and gets $29.90 as his answer. And we know that if this question needs you to add taxes after determining the final price, Joe Schmo is a libertarian who straight-up does not believe in taxes!

Standardized exams are not going anywhere, but educators do not have to treat these as drill-and-kill exercises that suck the life out of classrooms. We can prepare students for the rigors of testing while also creating rigorous and engaging critical thinking activities. Think about how you can leverage the Joe Schmo strategy to have students create their own multiple-choice responses to questions.

Joe Schmo becomes very helpful here. Too often, if we ask students to prepare their own multiple-choice responses to a question like the previous example, we get very ridiculous responses. Students would make the correct answer of $27 a choice. Their other three choices would be $40 million, –750,000, and rainbow. When we constrain their universe by asking them to only include responses that Joe Schmo can plausibly come up with, we are asking them to make reasonable predictions and inferences. We are helping them develop the habit of putting themselves in the shoes of others, again creating an opportunity to become more empathetic. Practically speaking, we are creating a world where students actually look forward to test prep season. I will discuss strategies for hacking standardized exams with critical thinking in more detail in Chapter 15.

# Examples of Mistake Analysis

## *Which Wrong Answer Is More "Right"?*

Which wrong answer is more "right" is a flexible method of infusing critical thinking into problem solving by allowing thinkers to evaluate the relative "rightness" of two or more incorrect solutions. Note that for the examples listed below, do not worry about redundancy! Doing mistake analysis every day is a very simple, repeatable, sustainable way to give students access to critical thinking on a regular basis. Project-based learning can be challenging to do even once a quarter, much less every day. But you can do *problem-based* learning multiple times per lesson.

**Math:** Create an example of the same problem answered in two different incorrect ways. A common trick would be to make one mistake based on a computational error and the other based on a conceptual misunderstanding. Once you set up the problem, you can divide the class into sides, with each set of students "representing" one of the incorrect solutions. As a differentiation strategy, you can assign the more challenging mistake to defend to your gifted and talented and higher-achieving students. You can also provide different levels of explanation or detail based on student ability as another differentiation strategy, enhancing rigor by having students predict the incorrect steps that led to the wrong answer. When you ask students to explain their answer, encourage them to find not only the most harmless interpretation of their error, but also the most egregious interpretation of the other side's.

The following is an example problem with two possible answers. Figure 8.3 includes explanations and justifications from each side.

Sula had eight apples. Her mother returned from an apple orchard with 48 apples and gave all of them to Sula. How many apples does Sula now have?

Person A's answer: Sula has 128 apples.

Person B's answer: Sula has 40 apples.

*Both of these answers are wrong. Which one is more "right?" Explain.*

**All subjects:** Instead of assigning test corrections after an exam (where it is common for students to just copy the right answers from a student who got it right), determine what the top 2–3 examples are

## FIGURE 8.3

*Detailed Example: Which Wrong Is More Right?*

|  | Person A | Person B |
|---|---|---|
| Less Detail | Sula has 128 apples. | Sula has 40 apples. |
| More Detail | 48<br>+8<br>———<br>128 | 48<br>−8<br>———<br>40 |
| Explanation of Error | Person A performed the correct operation but did not align the numbers using the correct place value. Person A's final answer is further away from the correct answer. | Person B did not perform the correct operation. But Person B computed accurately, recognizing the correct place value of the 8. |
| Why is your side more "right"? | Person A recognizes that if Sula's mother is giving her more apples, she should have more apples. Person B's conclusion that Sula somehow has less apples than she started out with is much farther off, logically. | Person B made a small mistake in reading the problem. Person B thought the problem was saying she started out with 8 apples and ended up with 48—so how many apples did Sula gain? Although Person B read the problem wrong, the answer was computed perfectly. Person A, however, lacks a basic understanding of simple addition. Person A could have counted on fingers and ended up with a more accurate answer. |

that students got wrong on the test and have students perform a Which Wrong Is More Right? analysis on those three questions as a way to recover lost points. In reviewing for a test, instead of giving students a massive packet, give them a smaller set of multiple-choice questions that your data has shown you students are still struggling with. You'll provide the correct answers for all of them, and students need to work on figuring out What Would Joe Schmo Do? to get each incorrect answer choice. You can go deeper by asking students to identify what was the *best* wrong answer (the one most students would end up picking incorrectly) and what was the *most* wrong answer (the one that was the most illogical to select).

**English Language Arts:** Use a similar technique as the math example, but create the mistakes based on two errors in grammar, essay organization, subject-verb agreement, etc. Look at a writing passage that has several errors, including punctuation, capitalization, and structure. Or look at three different paragraphs, one with poor grammar, one with bad organization, and one that was technically perfect but didn't actually answer the question. Have students evaluate which mistake is the most important and/or have them decide which writing should receive the highest score on your writing rubric.

**Science:** Analyze experiments with biased or flawed procedures likely to lead to unreliable data and have students analyze which experiment's outcomes will be most "right." The geocentric view of the universe is incorrect. But what is the best evidence for this (or any) scientific principle. For any topic where students are likely to make common errors, like confusing speed for velocity in physics or mixing up the difference between the properties of a plant cell and an animal cell in biology, creating What Would Joe Schmo Do? questions would always work.

**Social Studies:** Students can analyze two different pieces of propaganda on the same issue that both exaggerate and cherry-pick facts. They can defend which side is the most "accurate." In any case, a key practice will be assigning groups in advance and carefully considering the level of detail provided in each example as a differentiation strategy.

**Foreign Language:** Use Which Wrong Is More Right? for common verb conjugation issues, especially for irregular verbs. False cognates—words that look like their matching definition in one language but mean something very different in the other—are also ripe examples for What Would Joe Schmo Do? questions.

**Career and Technical Education:** In any CTE course that involves a safety-related procedure, documenting an incident report, making case notes, executing a cooking technique, performing an accounting task, or any rule-based activity that students commonly do not complete accurately (especially if in real-life, this is an area where even professionals in this field commonly make this error), have students look at two incorrect versions of the strategy and choose which incorrect version of the procedure is the most "right" and why.

# Note

1  Lubitz v. Wells,19 Conn. Supp. 322 (Conn. 1955).

# Chapter 9

# Investigation and Discovery

What the general public thinks courtroom lawyers do is different than what they actually do. Whether we are thinking about criminal or civil attorneys, everything we see on television and in movies portrays lawyers as constantly in the courtroom arguing, questioning witnesses on the stand, and making poetic opening and closing statements. In reality, the overwhelming majority of any criminal or civil case is spent on investigation and discovery.

This process models a very important part of learning and life: navigating the journey from a gut feeling to an informed opinion. As an adult, you might be thinking about buying a new car, taking your family on a trip to Disneyland, or trying out a new workout or exercise program. You typically have some general idea of where to start based on your existing knowledge, biases, preferences, and expertise—all part of what creates your "gut feeling." But the same way attorneys do not take their client's version of the story of the case as gospel, we need to ensure students have the tools to transition from having a gut feeling to formulating an informed opinion.

As educators, when we think about the critical thinking skills and dispositions we need to develop in our students, asking good questions is not enough. We also want to make sure students can ask good questions of

DOI: 10.4324/9781003482147-12

themselves. We want them to build research instincts, creating healthy voices inside their heads that ask questions like these:

Where do I start?
What do I know already?
What I do next?
How do I know that's true?
Why should I believe you?
What's really going on here?
What else do I need to know?

Let's use a familiar case from the early 1990s to model this process. If you happen to already know the facts of this case, pretend that you don't so you can attempt to experience the journey of growing from a gut feeling to an informed opinion.

## Too Hot to Handle

### Liebeck v. McDonald's Restaurants (1994)[1]

Chris took his 79-year-old grandmother, Stella, to McDonald's for a cup of coffee. Chris was the driver. They paid 49 cents for the coffee, and Chris pulled the car forward and pulled over (to a complete stop) so that his grandmother could add creamer and sugar to her cup. When Stella tried to remove the lid, she spilled the coffee all over her lap and was burned very badly. Stella sued McDonald's.

Before we do any analysis of this case, I want to press pause. Let's go back to the exact moment when Stella spilled the coffee on herself and explain, in detail, what happened in the next 30 minutes after this spill occurred. She probably went to the hospital, saw doctors, etc. But what happened immediately after?

Picture the scene. Chris and Stella go through the drive-through to get Stella's coffee. Chris pulls over so Stella can add cream and sugar to her cup. Stella spills the coffee. What is the next immediate action? If you think screaming, you are probably on the right track. Third-degree burns are typically so bad you can see bone. Does she just scream while she sits there in the car, covered with scalding hot coffee? No, she probably gets out of the car and is frantically trying to shake it off. What is happening around her while this is going on? We know she is in the parking lot, so there might be other people around. If this happened today, no doubt someone would be pulling out a cell phone to capture the scene on social media like, "Ooh, I'm about to go viral with this footage!" But in the early 1990s, with no cell phones, perhaps a bystander more quickly tries to help Stella.

What might this help look like? Maybe someone offers napkins. Maybe someone runs inside to tell the McDonald's manager, trying to get some sort of first aid. Hopefully someone calls 911. How is that call made? In the early 90s, someone could have one of those old-school giant cell phones or one of those unreliable, staticky car phones. But it's much more likely that this call is made using the landline phone at McDonald's. Does Chris even wait for the ambulance here? It depends, maybe, on how far away the hospital is. But presuming that Chris drives his grandmother to the hospital, what happens then? Do they give this 79-year-old woman a huge stack of paperwork and say "Have a seat. See you in three hours?" Probably not. Someone is probably giving Stella immediate care for her injury, even before a doctor sees her.

Pressing pause is powerful. Think about the cognitive skills employed by brainstorming what happened during the next 30 minutes. We are making several predictions and inferences. We are applying background knowledge to develop a complex, detailed potential timeline. This is no different than the type of brainstorming lawyers do when they first receive a case; all they know are small details from the client's version of what happened or the information on a police report. Pressing pause and brainstorming help build that critical thinking disposition where students will read a piece of text and say in their heads, "Uh oh. Please do not go in that cave. Nothing good is going to happen in that cave." Then, a few pages later, they'll say, "See! I told you not to go in that cave."

After pressing pause, we are now in a much better position to think through the McDonald's investigation. In civil litigation, the discovery period gives each side the chance to create and swap a list of witnesses, demand sets of evidence, and ask an initial set of questions to the opposing party. Witnesses are not limited to eyewitnesses. In fact, in a case like this, where there is not much doubt about what actually happened (Stella spilled coffee on herself, and the coffee burned her), we probably do not need an extensive list of eyewitnesses. Instead, we want to think about witnesses who can help Stella make the case that McDonald's caused her to suffer extreme pain and suffering because of reckless practices, policies, and procedures. McDonald's would want to have witnesses to show that there was nothing wrong with anything the company did internally and that, if anyone, Stella is the person who is at fault here.

When listing witnesses, the thinking should be (1) how will this witness's testimony impact the case, and (2) how might this witness be biased? Some witnesses might be less biased than others, but every witness will have some sort of bias. Starting with the witnesses, let's move past the most obvious ones. Clearly, Stella, Chris, the doctors who treated Stella, the employees present at the McDonald's, and other customers who may have been eyewitnesses in the parking lot or in the restaurant would be witnesses. Let's dig deeper. If you were Stella, what witnesses would you want to call up to prove that McDonald's was reckless here? To prove McDonald's was reckless, we would probably need to show that the coffee was too hot and that what McDonald's was doing was unsafe.

To get there, we could talk to an expert witness on coffee temperature. But experts can be too technical, so juries might not understand what they are talking about. Is there a more down-to-earth person who can help us out? How about someone from the company who makes the coffee machine itself? It would be super helpful to understand the proper way to use the machine and maintain it, and to compare the proper procedures to whatever procedures McDonald's used. The same applies for whoever made the cup and lid. Speaking to the minimum-wage employee who poured and served the coffee is probably less important than speaking to the person who teaches the coffee-making course at Hamburger University where McDonald's trains its managers.

To show the extent of injuries, we will certainly want to speak to the doctors who treated Stella's burns. But it might be more powerful to speak to Stella's primary care physician to understand her condition prior to this injury. We want to know if Stella was running marathons before this. We also want to know if she had arthritis in her hands or another condition, like Parkinson's disease, that could help us understand what may have caused this spill to happen.

We might need to get more creative. We might want to speak to other McDonald's coffee customers, especially those in Stella's age group. We definitely want to test out a few "evil" theories, like "what if McDonald's got tired of giving out the senior discount?" And we should not stop with McDonald's, but also speak to representatives from Burger King, Wendy's,

Starbucks, and even the local diner to find out how hot they keep their coffee.

Thinking of these witnesses will help lead us toward evidence we need to collect. We definitely want to see pictures of Stella's burns, spill patterns in Chris's car, and even what Stella was wearing that day. Was she wearing a fabric that would absorb a coffee spill more than other fabrics would? Was Stella wearing a miniskirt? The car was at a complete stop, but maybe we want to analyze it more closely to figure out if there was anything wrong with the passenger seat that might cause it to slide unexpectedly. We probably want McDonald's to provide a list of other people who suffered coffee burns and understand how McDonald's resolved these cases.

If we are representing McDonald's, we probably want to collect similar information from other competitors. We also want to know if Stella has any character issues that can call her claims into doubt. If Stella files a new frivolous lawsuit every month, this information would help us paint a negative picture of her.

Once we have a list of witnesses and physical evidence, rattling off questions becomes much easier. You probably had a million questions in your head from the time you heard the facts of this case. How hot was this coffee? Is there something wrong with Stella's skin that would lead to this type of burn? You can probably add on another five to seven questions for every one of the witnesses and about every piece of evidence you identified. Figure 9.1 is a template for recording information about witnesses, evidence, and questions.

Here is where it gets interesting. When an attorney for a party to a case makes these discovery requests and sends them out to the other party, the attorney rarely gets exactly what is asked for. Instead the opposing party provides just enough information from requesting documents, physical evidence, and interviewing witnesses to make you have even more questions than you started with. In this "too hot to handle" example, I am modeling this common practice by limiting the amount of information I reveal at this step. Here is what I am revealing at this time:

> The coffee Stella received was between 180–190°F. At that temperature, coffee can cause third-degree burns within seconds of touching the skin.
> This coffee was about 20 degrees hotter than other restaurants' coffee and 30 degrees hotter than coffee made at home.

**FIGURE 9.1**
*Blank Investigation Table*

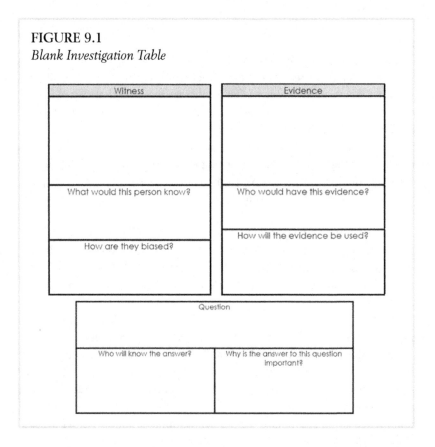

McDonald's had about 700 complaints about the temperature of its
coffee over the past 10 years before Stella's accident. These complaints specifically involved customers who suffered third-degree
burns from coffee spills.

The coffee caused Stella to suffer third-degree burns on over 16% of
her body, including her inner thighs and genitals. She was hospi-
talized for eight days, required skin grafts (in which skin is taken
from one part of the body and transplanted to another part), spent
two years recovering, and was permanently disfigured. While she
was injured, Stella lost more than 20 pounds, which dropped her
weight to 83 pounds.

Looking at the first two points about the temperature, what additional questions do you have? The question "why" might come to mind. Why in the world would McDonald's brew its coffee at temperatures so hot it would cause immediate burns? Why would it be substantially hotter than coffee at other restaurants? If we are representing McDonald's, maybe we're wondering if there are some valid reasons for this coffee being so hot. Maybe there is a valid, customer service-related reason. What if this incident occurred in Chicago in February? It would make sense that McDonald's might want coffee served at the drive-through to be hotter than normal because the second an employee sticks an arm out the window to pass off the coffee, the coffee is already exposed to very cold air.

The fact that 700 people had similar complaints of third-degree burns in the prior decade probably leads to another set of questions. We want to figure out what, if anything, McDonald's did in response to these complaints. We want to know how these complaints were disbursed geographically. Were these burns all from one McDonald's restaurant, from a small set of restaurants, or from McDonald's restaurants across the country? We would also want to investigate the timeline of these burns. It would be notable if a huge spike in complaints happened in the past two years after almost no complaints in the preceding eight years. Last, but certainly not least, can denominators get some love here? Seven hundred might sound like a large number. But what if McDonald's served 700 *trillion* cups of coffee in the last decade?

What questions do you have after learning the extent of Stella's injuries? Eight days of hospitalization, two years of recovery, skin grafts, and third-degree burns covering 16% of her body sound worse than you imagined for a coffee spill. You might start by trying to figure out what details about this incident made her injuries so severe. Did the other 700 people who suffered from third-degree burns also get burned this badly? You might want to ask the question I asked myself when I first learned of these facts: why did I automatically assume Stella's case was frivolous? I felt bad about my knee-jerk reaction to dismissing her case, and maybe you feel it, too. Reflecting on the differences between your gut reaction to this case and your reaction after starting to uncover the facts helps to further develop the healthy sense of skepticism we know is so important as a critical thinking disposition.

Now, we are at the last round of discovery. We are about to receive a brand new set of facts about this case. Here is what we know after the last round of discovery:

McDonald's sells millions of cups of coffee each year and did not consider 700 complaints over 10 years to be a significant number.

One of the reasons McDonald's coffee is so hot is that McDonald's realized that at extremely high temperatures, they can brew the same strength of coffee using a lower quantity of beans.

Stella originally just asked for $20,000 to cover her medical expenses. McDonald's, which was already a global company worth billions, offered her only $800.

By the end of the actual trial, the jury was so mortified by McDonald's conduct that it awarded Stella $200,000 in damages for her injuries, which a judge reduced by $40,000 after finding Stella 20% liable for her injury. The jury also awarded Stella $2.7 million dollars in punitive damages as a deterrent to future misconduct not just by McDonald's but also by other restaurants that might otherwise put profits over consumer safety. The presiding judge later reduced Stella's total damages to $640,000. By that time, though, the probusiness lobby had already impacted public sentiment by making a mockery of this case. Because the general public would not look past its knee-jerk assessment, this case led to reforms in the United States civil litigation system that made it much harder for people to bring legitimate claims.

The thinkLaw strategy of Investigation and Discovery has tremendous implications as an instructional strategy. Imagine if instead of revealing these facts slowly as I did in this process, I just decided to not reveal them. You probably would not be too happy because you had built up anticipation and wanted to hear what came next. You were yearning for learning. I could have simply asked you to read a three-paragraph passage about the McDonald's hot coffee lawsuit and then to answer five questions about it. But I purposely created a greater sense of intrigue. Investigation and Discovery models that sensation of flipping through channels on a TV. You stumble across the first two minutes of an episode of one of the many detective shows on the air at any given time. The moment you see the jogger find a body in a bush, you realize that you have just waved goodbye to the next 58 minutes of your life.

This process is an exemplar of a low-floor, high-ceiling model of inquiry that raises the bar for all learners. When you give students the opportunity to press pause and make inferences and predictions, it increases their drive to go deeper into their learning. The "Hot Coffee" case was a thorough example meant to demonstrate the potential for Investigation and Discovery as a practical critical thinking strategy. But as you will see in the subject-area examples that follow, you can see powerful impact to your students' ability to access critical thinking by just using bite-sized pieces of this strategy.

# Examples of Investigation and Discovery

Here are some practical ideas for incorporating this strategy into your classroom.

## English and Language Arts

"Press pause" while reading to ask students to make predictions and inferences about what might happen next. This strategy is particularly effective when authors use foreshadowing. Start reading a poem or book from the last line or last page as a strategy to get students to work backward to predict the beginning and middle of a piece based on the ending. Have students write or tell stories entirely based on the images of a picture book before they read the book or have the book read to them. When learning new grammar rules like parallel sentence structure, have students predict what they think the grammatical rule is, and give them more examples of what is a proper use of parallel sentence structure and what is not until they can articulate what the rule is.

## Math

For any math vocabulary word that can be understood through patterns and trends, like functions, prime numbers, or square roots, use discovery to get students to predict the definition. For instance, you can create the following gradual release of information followed by the corresponding questions:

Information: 3 is a prime number. 5 is a prime number. 7 is a prime number.

Question: What is the definition of a prime number? (Students will probably presume that a prime number is an odd number.)

Information: 9 is a composite number. 11 is a prime number. 13 is a prime number. 15 is a composite number.

Question: What is the definition of a prime number? What is the definition of a composite number? (Students will probably notice that 9 and 15 both have factors other than 1, while 11 and 13 do not. But at this point students might presume that both prime and composite numbers have to be odd numbers.)

Information: 4 is a composite number. 6, 8, 10, 12 and 14 are also composite numbers. 17 is a prime number.

Question: What is the definition of a prime number? What is the definition of a composite number? Have you changed any of your definitions? Why or why not? (Students will probably keep their definition the same as before, but maybe add in a detail explaining that even numbers are always composite numbers.)

Information: 0 is neither prime nor composite. 1 is neither prime nor composite. 2 is prime.

Question: What is the definition of a prime number? What is the definition of a composite number? Why are 0 and 1 neither prime nor composite? Have you changed any of your definitions? Why or why not? (This example will force students to question their initial assumptions that 0 and 2 are even numbers but neither is composite. They also have to figure out what makes 0 and 1 neither prime nor composite.)

The "a-ha" moments students get as their assumptions are challenged throughout this process make the definitions of prime and composite numbers far "stickier."

## Social Studies

When studying a war, use an incomplete timeline and ask students to predict conflicts that happened in the leadup to the war.

History is filled with negotiations between parties that did not always have complete information. For instance, consider the Louisiana Purchase and France's decision to sell this territory to the United States at a surprisingly low price point. Turn this event into an investigation as to why France would agree to such a deal. Students could identify potential witnesses they would want to speak to, key documents they would want to analyze, and important questions they would want to ask. Then, similar to the "Hot Coffee" case, slowly unveil the contributing factors leading to this sale, including the Haitian Revolution.

## Science and Career and Technical Education

Students can analyze any phenomenon, like a chemical reaction, a plant growing, the Earth getting warmer, etc., and predict what is causing it to occur as a hook to learning about the issues.

Instead of classifying igneous, metamorphic, and sedimentary rock by memorizing definitions, have students analyze different types of rocks and classify them into groups on their own. You can ask them to look for key characteristics, like crystals, glassy surfaces, ribbon/stripe-like layers, gas bubbles, and sand or pebbles. Once they start to sort these rocks into categories, there's a much better chance they will remember the properties of the three different types of rocks because of the deeper appreciation that comes from learning the rules through the experimentation process. A similar discovery process can be used for any topic in Career and Technical Education.

## Foreign Language

Students can watch a conversation between two people speaking a foreign language using some combination of unknown vocabulary and unknown concepts, and based on mood, body language, and pre-existing knowledge of vocabulary, they can predict what they believe the conversation was about. Then, once you teach the concept and new vocabulary, students can piece together the story bit by bit as if they were cracking a case.

## Fine Arts

For any genre, era, or style of art or music, you can have students classify like groups and determine the characteristics of what makes each of these alike. Then you can provide more information and details about what makes a piece from the Baroque Era sound Baroque, what makes an impressionist piece of art impressionist, etc.

## *Physical Education*

In the Investigations and Discovery framework, pressing pause is the same as calling a time out. During any activity, pressing pause to ask students what they think will happen next can be a great way to get students to practice making predictions and inferences. For instance, if in a three-on-three basketball game students are moving towards the left side of the basket but using their right hands, pressing pause to have students explain the technical error could be a helpful teaching moment. This would also apply to any technique in any sport or activity, especially in weight-training, when an important safety issue is at play.

## Note

1  Liebeck v. McDonald's Restaurants (N.M. Dist. Ct. 1994).

# Chapter 10

# Settlement and Negotiation

Think about the last time you told a young person, "You should be a lawyer." What caused you to say that? Often, we tell children who love to argue and who never stop talking that they should be lawyers. We could not be more wrong.

In both civil and criminal law, the overwhelming majority of cases never go to trial. They settle. So, the students we should be tapping to pursue a law degree are those who are always in the mix of other students' conflicts. You know those students: the girl who always appoints herself as the negotiator-in-chief for other drama that has nothing to with her; the boy who is a natural mediator everyone comes to in times of conflict. This settlement instinct goes to the essence of learning how to disagree without being disagreeable. We often refer to skills like being able to find common ground as "soft skills," but these are some of the hardest skills to teach.

The following is a real-life legal case to help explain how the thinkLaw strategy of Settlement and Negotiation translates to a practical framework for critical thinking.

DOI: 10.4324/9781003482147-13

# The Barking Dogs

Karen and John live in Oregon and own several dogs (Green, 2017). They also raise chickens and other animals at their home. Their dogs are Tibetan Mastiffs and weigh more than 150 pounds. These dogs are also very loud and start barking around 5:00 a.m. every morning and continue through the day. Dale and Debra are their neighbors, who lived in their home before Karen, John, and their Tibetan mastiffs moved next door. Dale and Debra have trouble sleeping and cannot get any quiet moments in their home because of the loud barking. Animal control has already punished the dog owners for noise violations, but the dog owners did not stop the noise. After a few years, the neighbors sue the dog owners because of the loud barking. The neighbors ask the Court to force the dog owners to get rid of their dogs and pay more than $200,000 for the damages caused by the loud dog barking over the last few years. If you were the dog owners, how might you try to settle this case?

Unsurprisingly, the most common response that students suggest is to tell the neighbors to move—never mind the fact that the neighbors lived there first. Without a framework in place for negotiating conflicts like this, it is so easy to get stuck in this limited, binary pattern. The tendency to argue "get rid of your dogs" or "if you don't like it, leave!" is par for the course given the state of discourse in our society. Fortunately, the DIM Process, a three-step system to open up investigations, helps create much more creative, out-of-the-box solutions to tough conflicts.

# The DIM Process

1. Determine the issues and ask "why" until you can determine the underlying interests.
2. Identify the most realistic, best possible outcome if you fail to reach a settlement (your BATNA, or best alternative to a negotiated agreement).
3. Make a creative offer that addresses the underlying interests in a way that exceeds your BATNA.

To practice this process, imagine that you are a building manager operating a tall office building in New York City. Tenants who work there complain every single day about how slow your elevators are, but replacing them with faster models could cost you millions of dollars. You'd have to pull expensive permits and deal with all sorts of asbestos issues, and it could put your building out of commission. But you want to resolve this issue. Let's start with identifying issues and interests.

The issue is the most obvious, immediate, surface-level problem. In this case, the building tenants' most obvious, immediate, surface-level problem is that the elevators are simply too slow. Moving beyond issues to interests requires us to ask why the issue truly matters to the impacted party. Why do tenants of this office building care that the elevators are so slow? It's not like people are all that eager to get to work. Put yourself in the shoes of someone who works in this building. You get to work and push the button for the elevator. It is super slow. Why does that slowness bother you? Because all you are doing is standing there, waiting. It's boring. You feel impatient and just generally annoyed with the wait.

If, instead of trying to solve the issue of the elevator being so slow, you focused on the interest of making the wait less boring, you can find some creative solutions. You can install mirrors on the outside and inside of elevators so that tenants can make sure they are looking sharp for the day instead of waiting impatiently. You can play music in the elevators as well. Will it be gangster rap or punk rock? Nope, Kenny G! Good ol' smooth jazz to take the edge off a bit. The DIM Process in action almost always yields more creative, workable solutions than the standard head-to-head style of dispute resolution people often use as a default.

With this strategy in mind, let's look at the facts of this case one more time (Green, 2017):

> Karen and John live in Oregon and own several dogs.
> They also raise chickens and other animals at their
> home. Their dogs are Tibetan Mastiffs and weigh more
> than 150 pounds. These dogs are also very loud and
> start barking around 5:00 a.m. every morning and
> continue through the day. Dale and Debra are their
> neighbors. Dale and Debra have trouble sleeping and
> cannot get any quiet moments in their home because of
> the loud barking. Animal control has already punished
> the dog owners for noise violations, but the dog owners
> did not stop the noise. After a few years, the neighbors
> sue the dog owners because of the loud barking. The

neighbors ask the Court to force the dog owners to get
rid of their dogs and pay more than $200,000 for the
damages caused by the loud dog barking over the last
few years. If you were the dog owners, how might you
try to settle this case?

To start the process, we want the dog owners to identify the neighbors'
issues and interests. The most obvious, immediate, surface-level problem
bothering the neighbors is the incessant barking. But why does the barking bother them? We can presume that if the dogs are barking all of the
time, the neighbors cannot sleep. The dogs wake them up, and the barking
makes it tough for them to concentrate. But why does this really bother
them? What is the underlying interest here? It might have something to
do with the neighbors' sense of home, generally. Most people have a basic
expectation that in their home they can enjoy a sense of peace and quiet.
So that's their interest: maintaining a sense of peace and quiet.

If the dog owners honestly assessed their BATNA, they would quickly
realize that this might not work out well for them. The dog owners have
already been penalized for noise violations. If the dog owners cannot
reach a deal, their track record will likely result in harsh treatment by the
court and a potential jury. A realistic assessment of their BATNA would
probably acknowledge that they will definitely end up in the wrong here
and have to pay for it. Maybe the fine will not end up being as high as
$200,000, but it might be significant. There is also a fair risk that the own-
ers will have to get rid of their dogs. If they are thinking carefully about
their interest in keeping their livestock safe and secure, as their attorneys,
the BATNA is so unfavorable that going to trial over this is probably not
worth the risk.

To make an opening offer, we want to think about how we can help the
neighbors obtain peace and quiet without the owners having to get rid of
the dogs and without paying $200,000. Maybe the owners can pay for the
dogs to be trained to not bark indiscriminately all day and all night. We
might be able to work out a deal with the neighbors where the owners pay
for them to have better sound insulation and soundproof windows at their
house. The key is, we now have options that did not exist when we only
focused on their issues.

In real life, this case had shocking outcomes. The Oregon jury awarded
more than $200,000 in damages to the neighbors and forced the dog
owners to "debark" their dogs—a surgery that involves modifying a dog's

vocal cords so the dog barks at a lower volume. If the dog owners did not want the dogs debarked, they had to get rid of them. This could have been avoided if the dog owners were willing to try the DIM Process to resolve the conflict.

In a world where teachers are asked to teach social-emotional learning on top of their other extensive responsibilities, the DIM Process is a convenient timesaver. The choice between rigorous academics and social-emotional learning is a false choice. Teaching our students powerful conflict negotiation skills helps them disagree without being disagreeable and work much more effectively as collaborators and problem solvers in a group context.

## Examples of Settlement and Negotiation

Here are several strategies to use the DIM Process as an instructional framework for critical thinking. Each one of these strategies requires students to identify the surface-level issues and then probe deeply into the "why" to determine the interests.

## *English Language Arts*

Develop alternative endings to novels and short stories that fulfill the characters' interests. For instance, in *Of Mice and Men*, ask students to think about what other options George could have considered to put Lennie out of his misery. However, students should not just randomly make up a new ending like, "A spaceship comes and takes Lennie back to Mars because he is really an alien from outer space." A valid alternative ending needs to satisfy the underlying interests of both parties. George's issue at the end of the book is his extreme frustration with Lennie. But why is George so frustrated? Probably because since the beginning of the novel, George has had to put up with so many of Lennie's issues. They just left another town because of one of Lennie's mistakes. George is tired of having to spend all of this time taking care of Lennie just for Lennie to keep on making the same mistakes over and over again. What alternative solutions could have allowed George to fulfill his interest?

## Social Studies

Ask students to determine the terms and conditions of a peace treaty that could have prevented a war by satisfying the underlying interests of both sides.

## Math

Problem-solving habits and mindsets are one of the most important, but often overlooked, aspects of solving challenging math and science problems. Often, when a student struggles with a specific math problem, the issue sounds like, "I'm stuck" or "I don't know how to do this." But helping students probe deeper with questions like "why am I stuck?" builds clarity around the metacognition process. Additionally, this process of thinking out loud helps students to develop a problem-solving strategy.

Take the following example:

Solve for N, O, V, and A (each represents a different digit)
$$\begin{array}{r} NOVA \\ \times\ A \\ \hline AVON \end{array}$$

The conversation I would encourage and explicitly teach students to have in their head sounds like this:

I'm stuck.
*Why am I stuck?* Because I don't know what N, O, V, and A are.
*Are there any clues?* Not that I see.
*What if I knew what I was doing? What would be my first step?* I think I would solve for A.
*Why?* Because there are three As in the problem, and A is the multiplier.
*Do I know anything about A?* No.
*Do I know what A is not?* Yes! A cannot be 0 or 1, because NOVA times 0 is 0, and NOVA times 1 would be NOVA.
*So, what do I think A is?*

As you can see, using probing questions to convert issues to interests is also a powerful, practical method of getting students to be intentional about their metacognition to work through the feeling of being stuck.

## Science

The Settlement and Negotiation process can be used to deepen students' understanding of any topic involving pseudo-science. In a unit on the earth, for instance, the DIM Process can be used to debate a flat-earther.

# Chapter 11

# Competition

Law school professors approach grading much differently than professors at the undergraduate and graduate level do. In graduate school, if students do the readings and write solid papers, they get an A. You show what you know, and you're good to go! Law school grading is different in two important ways. First, law school professors grade students on a mandatory curve. This means that in any given class of 30 students, 100% of students can demonstrate a mastery of important legal concepts and principles, but the mandatory curve may set the median grade at a B– and explicitly limit the number of A grades a professor can distribute. Second, professors blindly grade law school exams. This means that most law school professors sort these exams in order from best to worst and then let the curve do its work.

To rise to the top, it is not enough to know the law. If all students do is regurgitate statutes and legal rules, they will probably earn a C–. If they do a decent job of applying facts to the law with pretty good analysis, they will fall squarely within a B range. To earn a coveted A, they need to stand out with exceptional analysis. And to win what is called the CALI award in a course, they have to write the best overall essay response compared to their classmates. They need to see the details and angles that no one else can see. They need to go beyond answering the question of "what" the

DOI: 10.4324/9781003482147-14

outcome should be. A-graded exams explain the "why" of the outcome, incorporating the public policy implications.

There are real consequences to the rat race of law school grades, at least in the short term. Most law schools only provide rankings to students who are in the top third of their classes. Several law school academic scholarships are contingent upon remaining in this top third group. Eligibility for law journals, which are a badge of prestige for law students, is also often determined by grades. Many of the highest-paying and most prestigious law firm opportunities and judicial clerkships are reserved for students in the top 5%–10% of their classes.

As a student, I underachieved in the K–12 system, throughout my undergraduate experience as a computer science major, and again in graduate school when I earned my master's in public administration. Law school was different. Not only did I graduate at the top of my class, earning several A's along the way, but I also got the CALI award in five different classes: Contracts, Constitutional Law, Property, Divorce Mediation, and Wills, Trusts, and Estates.

My motivation did not come from a desire to get good grades because I never cared about grades. Instead, I was fired up by the idea that my creativity counted, that my mistakes—spending my whole life messing things up and saying, "Well, what had happened was..."—were now an asset. Law school rejected the norm of what it meant to be a good student. Law school rarely involved any homework assignments or busywork. I was rarely graded for participation. It did not matter how neat my notebook was. It wasn't about how much I could memorize; it was about thinking on my toes. Law school turned out to be a crucial competition with myself.

When I used the DRAAW+C process on my final exams, it felt like I was playing both sides of a chessboard. There was an intrinsic thrill involved in putting the debating voices in my head onto paper. I honestly never worried about how I would stack up against others. I just wanted to do the best I could to fulfill my personal sense of accomplishment.

This is the type of competition educators do not see enough. When we think of competition in our society, we think of sports, academic competitions, spelling bees, and class rankings. Who's the best? And we shame the idea of participation trophies because "everyone's a winner" does not fit into our idea of what competition is. This creates a world where young people who do not buy into this model are labeled as lazy. We say they need more grit or they lack that hunger, fire, or desire. But in my struggle with "I don't care" syndrome, I realized that certain types of competition are simply not motivating.

If I had to have a three-point shootout with Stephen Curry, play Serena Williams in a tennis match, or have a no-holds-barred spell-off with the national spelling champ, I am not going to be motivated. I would feel too outclassed. But if the competitive energy comes from a more intrinsic sense of purpose, it feels totally different. Can I make several three-point shots in a row? Can I do ten tennis serves in a row without a double fault? Can I spell the championship words from the last three national spelling bee finals? If you put an age-appropriate puzzle in front of someone, it is almost impossible for that person to not start piecing it together. Competition focused on this type of intrinsic motivation is the last thinkLaw strategy discussed in this book.

## Should Student Athletes Be Paid

Speaking of competition, one of the most controversial questions in college sports used to be whether we should pay college athletes. This question is typically applied to athletes at Division I schools in the two biggest revenue-generating sports, men's basketball and football. Since the publication of the first edition of this book, drastic changes have taken place in the college sports landscape allowing athletes to receive all kinds of monetary benefits for their names, images, and likenesses (NIL). But it is still useful to think through the critical thinking process of what led to this outcome.

The NCAA, or National Collegiate Athletic Association, oversees most college athletics. The NCAA says that in the United States only about 2% of high school athletes are awarded scholarships, and not all of those scholarships cover the complete costs of a college education (NCAA, 2018). The NCAA also reports that very few college athletes get to move on to play professional sports and that the greatest benefit for student athletes is to receive their college degree for little or no money. College athletes have to be amateur athletes, which means they cannot be paid. They do receive scholarship money to cover specific expenses, but athletes do not have a choice of how to use the money.

The NCAA made a $10.8 billion contract with CBS in 2010. This contract meant that CBS could show the men's basketball tournament on TV until 2024 (Wolverton, 2010) and this contract has since been extended until 2032 for an additional $8.8 billion. Five hundred thirty-five coaches from the largest schools made a total of $440 million while the colleges gave $426 million in scholarships to 20,000 players (Isadore, 2016). On average, these coaches make $823,000 per year while a student-athlete only receives roughly $20,000 per year in aid. Universities can also make deals with athletic companies. For example, in 2014 Notre Dame made a ten year deal with Under Armour for $90 million.

Should student athletes be paid? In the typical academic exercise relating to this issue, students would go about answering the question the same way they always have. They would use the DRAAW+C framework to walk away with a persuasive response that makes a definitive claim supported by a logical rule, considers arguments on both sides of the debate, and weighs the public policy consequences of their decision. Although there is intrinsic motivation in doing an exercise like this because it involves issues of fairness and justice, competition can also be leveraged here.

In this example, only a few details are provided about this case. Instead of asking students to read a longer passage of facts or research on their own, educators can "press pause" and play the Argument-Counterargument Game instead. Here, regardless of each student's individual viewpoint, the student receives an argument and has to develop a strong counterargument for that same exact point. For example, a student might receive the following argument against paying student athletes: *College athletes get free access to excellent coaching, facilities, and training, giving them an opportunity to be a professional player that they would not get otherwise.* But the student now has to develop a counterargument to this point that directly undermines it, such as:

> If you look at how few college athletes go on to play professionally, the free coaching and training that student athletes receive does not lead to a valuable outcome for the vast majority of college athletes. Besides, young athletes can often gain opportunities to play overseas and skip college altogether, getting paid while also receiving the same training and coaching benefits that student athletes would.

The Argument-Counterargument Game is not just great for competition based on intrinsic motivation. It is also a practical way to incorporate meaningful discussions around controversial topics in your classrooms

(see Figure 11.1 for example arguments). At a time when it is more important than ever to create spaces to help students process the issues of the
day, no teacher wants to end up on the news because a classroom discussion went off the rails. The structure of the Argument-Counterargument
Game allows you to create healthy boundaries for a discussion. Giving

## FIGURE 11.1
*Arguments for and Against Paying Student Athletes*

| Arguments in Favor of Paying Student Athletes | Arguments Against Paying Student Athletes |
|---|---|
| Many student athletes spend 40-60 hours a week with their sport. On top of that, they have to go to class and complete homework. It is impossible for them to have jobs. The scholarships cover their academic expenses, but they have no way to earn spending money. | College athletes have access to high-quality coaching, top-notch facilities, and high-level training for free. If a player has the potential to turn into a professional player, the preparation they will receive from the college program will be very valuable. |
| There are very strict rules for college athletes when it comes to opportuni-ties to make money. College athletes are not allowed to sign endorsement deals. An endorsement deal means that they would get part of the money when their name is used on a jersey or their likeness is used in a video game or their picture is on a poster. | A college athlete's job is to be a student. They are not employees of the school. They are not professional sports players. In college, sports are extracurricular activities. They can earn a bachelor's degree, and some-times a master's degree, without ending up in a lot of debt. |
| There are a lot of jobs that have been created from college sports. A few include: coaching staff, personal trainers, ticket salespeople, and referees. The NCAA employs over 500 people. All of these people are making money from college sports. Everyone is being paid except the athletes who are the stars of the games. | There are universities that make a lot of money from their sports programs. Texas A&M has made as much as $180 million dollars in a school year. But a lot of schools don't make nearly that much money. Around 44% of colleges and uni-versities make less than $20 million dollars a year from their sports programs. Those schools couldn't afford to pay their athletes like the bigger schools. |

students the opportunity to argue different sides during this game helps them to appreciate alternative viewpoints and dispute the idea, not the person. This process accelerates the challenging task of learning to disagree without being disagreeable.

## The Four Corners Game

Another way to "press pause" and have students leverage competition as a critical thinking strategy is the Four Corners Game. To use this strategy, introduce an excerpt or short summary of the issue at hand. Then, have students take the rest of the information as it comes in and sort it into four categories: In Favor, Against, Irrelevant, and Goes Either Way (see Figure 11.2). The following section is an example of how this works.

## No Take Backs: Williams v. Walker-Thomas Furniture Co. (1965)

Ora needed to buy some furniture. She went to Walker-Thomas Furniture Store to purchase what she needed on a payment plan. Between 1957 and 1962, Ora purchased 13 different items that totaled $1,500. Ora signed the payment plan contract. The contract contained language that allowed the furniture store to take back all of the furniture Ora purchased if Ora missed even one payment. Ora fell behind on her payments. Walker-Thomas Furniture took back all of the furniture items Ora had ever purchased. Should Walker-Thomas Furniture be allowed to take back all of Ora's purchases?

There is enough information immediately to make a gut decision. But it is challenging to conduct a thorough analysis and reach a conclusion

FIGURE 11.2
*The Four Corners Game*

| Yes | No |
|---|---|
| Irrelevant | Goes Either Way |

without more information. Instead of having students read a long passage with all of the facts, cut out fact strips (see Figure 11.3) and have them organize them into one of the four corners. This is an interesting activity to leave up to students to organize on their own. If they start sorting right away, they will likely find themselves changing the sorting as they go. For example, "Ora lived on a government-provided income of $218 a month" might seem completely irrelevant at first. But when thinkers learn that the stereo cost $514 and that the salesperson knew Ora only made $218 a month, this becomes a fact that may end up supporting the case against Walker-Thomas Furniture.

On the surface, the Four Corners Game might not seem like a competitive process. But there is an inherent competition of ideas that naturally develops in any sort of classification exercise. For instance, look at the following fact: "In 1962, Ora still owed 3 cents on her 1957 purchase. Walker-Thomas wanted to take back the items from that purchase." There is a strong argument that Walker-Thomas's actions seem way too harsh here. But there is also an argument that if Ora did not want her furniture taken away, she should not have missed her payments. This fact could go either way, but it can also land squarely within a specific corner for or against Walker-Thomas.

### FIGURE 11.3
*Fact Strips*

| | |
|---|---|
| Ora was a single mother of seven children. | Ora lived on a government-provided income of $218 a month. |
| Walker-Thomas Furniture never gave Ora a copy of the contract she signed. | The payment plan was set up in a manner where as long as Ora had a balance, she always owed money on her old purchases. |
| In 1962, Ora still owed 3 cents on her 1957 purchase. Walker-Thomas wanted to take back the items from that purchase. | As long as Ora kept buying new items she would never be able to fully pay off the items she already had. |
| In 1962, a door-to-door salesperson sold Ora a stereo for $514. | The door-to-door salesperson that sold Ora the stereo knew that Ora was on public assistance and had a monthly income of $218. |

This process is not about being "right," but about persuasion and the accomplishment of piecing together a complex puzzle. We live in a time when academic pressure leads to more cheating than educators would ever want to admit. But with activities like the Four Corners Game, thinkers don't, won't, and can't cheat. If you have six groups working on this activity, you will get six different responses.

# Quick and Short Competition

As someone with years of experience in the classroom, I understand the reality of teaching. Despite our best efforts, every single lesson is not going to be a masterpiece in critical thinking. We are not here to entertain students every single waking moment they are in front of us. Some days, we have to teach the quadratic formula, and teaching the quadratic formula for the first time is exactly as compelling as it sounds.

Without a base level understanding of core concepts, deep critical thinking within the specific context of a discipline or context is challenging, if not impossible, for students. However, this does not mean that the entire instructional block must be dreadful. There are ways to seamlessly integrate quick and short critical thinking activities that encourage the positive aspects of competition without taking away the crucial time needed to cover core concepts.

Whenever you know your instruction will be heavy on content, consider weaving short critical thinking games, questions, and activities into the first five minutes of class as part of your bell-ringer, warmup, or whatever you call it. This way, you can grab your students' attention immediately, give them time to practice the habit of critical thinking on a regular basis, and create a positive energy for learning, which is crucial for a day when you know a lot of learning is going on.

These competitive games grounded in critical thinking are also great for short brain breaks in the middle of a lesson. Say that you just finished walking third graders through an analysis of an abstract poem. None of us have to be third graders to understand what that energy might feel like. Breaking up the pace by introducing one of these short activities before your next transition revives your students, refocuses their minds, and, again, gives them practice regularly accessing the habit of critical thinking.

There are countless games, puzzles, logic problems, and riddles that can be used. My favorites to use are the 24 Game, Word Puzzles (or Wuzzles), and What is This?

# The 24 Game

The 24 Game (https://www.24game.com) is one of my favorite games ever—not just because I live by the "once a mathlete, always a mathlete" mantra, but because even students who don't "do" math are driven by the complex problem solving involved in this process. The concept of the 24 Game is that the player must use all four numbers on each card to reach the result of 24, using any combination of addition, subtraction, multiplication, and division (Suntex International Inc., 2019). There are one-dot, two-dot, and three-dot problems (three-dot problems are the most challenging), which allow teachers to differentiate for students based on their level of ability. For instance, if the four numbers were 8, 8, 3, and 1, there would be at least three ways to get to 24:

You can do: $3 + 1 = 4$, $4 \times 8 = 32$, and $32 - 8 = 24$.
Or you can go with: $3 - 1 = 2$, $2 \times 8 = 16$, and $16 + 8 = 24$.
Or, if you are feeling like the mathlete of the year, you can try: $8 + 1 = 9$, $9 \div 3 = 3$, and $3 \times 8 = 24$.

There are several ways to set up this activity. One option is to put one of these problems on the board for students to solve and see who gets the answer first. However, this may discourage students who are less quick on their feet from participating fully. A better way to approach this is to try putting up three of these cards that are all at different levels of difficulty. Instead of seeing who is "done" first, you can make the competition about how many ways the problem can be solved. In a secondary class, you can turn this into a competition based on how the whole class does relative to other class periods. In elementary grades, you can set up the competition based on mixed-ability groups. This evens the playing field and pushes everyone to work to their potential. Students who struggle will be focusing on getting just the one-dot problem solved to get at least one point for their group. But our 24 Game all-stars will likely focus on figuring out as many ways as possible to complete the hardest examples.

## Word Puzzles (Wuzzles)

Word Puzzles have been intriguing to me since the days of the television game show *Classic Concentration*. This was a show that combined matching (which is its own form of *The Hunger Games* in my household when I play it with my children) with translating visual images into common phrases. Wuzzles work because they involve a lot of talking out loud and verbalizing metacognition. Students are also typically unafraid to say the wrong answer in these problems, because they recognize that the wrong answer gets them to where they want to be.

Figure 11.4 includes some examples of Wuzzles that you can seamlessly integrate into the start of your class or use as a brain break.

The goal here is to look at the words and how they are arranged to figure out what common phrase the Wuzzle represents. Starting with the

FIGURE 11.4
*Examples of Wuzzles*

top left, you see "drawn scale scale" with one "drawn" and two "scales." The answer is "drawn to scale." Get it? Great, now I will give you a "round of applause." Call it magic or critical thinking—it doesn't matter either way. You're basically just "splitting hairs." The best part about doing these is that when it comes to looking for the information you need, "they're all the same." There are endless options for Wuzzles all over the Internet. You might think about the options and say wow, "there's no end to it." And there is lots of choice involved here, which is great because you know what they say: "different strokes for different folks."

## What Is This?

This is a brain break you can do in just a few seconds if you'd like. Simply search online for "close-up picture of _____" (be careful of what you use for the blank). Then, in the midst of covering content, ask your students to tell you, "What is this?" See Figure 11.5 for an example.

Students often start to think creatively of what they may be looking at. Some might see a feather—a beehive, even. Some might correctly guess that this is an orange. Here is where your sly poker face and misleading questioning can really mess with their heads. Using your most skeptical voice, ask, "Are you certain this is an orange? Please make sure you are looking at this closely." See the close-up next to its answer in Figure 11.6.

This questioning technique is even more powerful when the answer seems more straightforward. The image in Figure 11.7 is a spider's leg. Students see this and automatically see that it is a spider. But try leading with the framing question, "The next one can be very tricky. Be very careful not to fall for the trick so many others fall for. Look very closely. What is this?" You will get to play all sorts of mind games.

After making tons of random, incorrect guesses like "a hairy arm on a very skinny person" or "a hairy, bent tree branch," students will have to reckon with the reality that they were tricked (see the answer in Figure 11.8). It is then helpful to inquire why they were so quick to doubt their instincts; it is one thing to have a healthy sense of skepticism, but when students look at a picture, analyze it, and make the educated conclusion that the close-up picture is the leg of a spider, why should they doubt it? Given what educators know about how confidence impacts our students'

**FIGURE 11.5**
*Close-Up Picture 1*

**FIGURE 11.6**
*Close-Up Picture 1 With Answer*

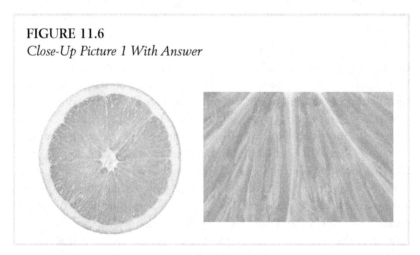

attitudes toward answering questions and taking risks, this is a powerful example to model the disposition of intellectual maturity. In other words, students should know that it is okay to feel secure in their answer when they have based that answer on a careful process of analytical reasoning.

**FIGURE 11.7**
*Close-Up Picture 2*

**FIGURE 11.8**
*Close-Up Picture 2 With Answer*

Someone saying, "I don't know about that"—with no additional insight, analysis, evidence, or details—should not be enough to make critical thinkers doubt their conclusions.

# PART III

## Practical Considerations for a Critical Thinking Revolution

# Chapter 12

# Making thinkLaw Work

Over the last several years, I have had the pleasure to train thousands of gifted and talented teachers on these thinkLaw strategies. Teachers are typically thrilled to have a tangible set of tools they can apply immediately to raise the levels of rigor and engagement in their classrooms. This applies especially to gifted and talented teachers who teach in a self-contained program or those who teach gifted students in a pull-out program for a specific amount of time each week. These teachers understand that their primary job is to unleash the full potential of all of their learners, and they typically have a solid foundation of instructional tools to do so. It also helps that their classes consist of nothing but gifted and talented students.

As exciting as it has been to hear that teachers of gifted and talented students are able to successfully implement thinkLaw strategies in their classrooms across the country, this is not the case for students in all classrooms. I have trained tens of thousands of general education teachers from every type of school imaginable. More often than I care to admit, certain groups of teachers report back to me that they struggle to use thinkLaw for all of their students. Teachers have told me how challenging it is to use thinkLaw strategies for ELLs. They have shared that students in special education have struggled with these types of activities, and students who

DOI: 10.4324/9781003482147-16

were not on grade level were considered "too low" to engage in these critical thinking frameworks.

This feedback made me realize that even if educators understand why critical thinking matters and have practical thinkLaw strategies to do it, they still need practical frameworks to ensure that they know how to teach critical thinking to *all* students. To be even clearer, it is one thing to teach critical thinking to all students; it is an entirely different goal to ensure that students are actually learning the critical thinking skills and dispositions that are being taught.

Several examples of the gap between teaching critical thinking and learning it come to mind. One October, I observed a middle school math teacher who was sick and tired of feeling like he had to guide students through each and every step of word problems. So, he put a complex word problem on the board and told students, "You got this! You can figure this out." One minute passed. Five minutes passed. Fifteen minutes passed. When time was up, all but two students had a blank page.

This reminded me of a time I included the following question on the first math exam of the year: "If you were a gambler, would you prefer to know the odds or probability of an event happening? Explain your preference." Most of my students skipped the question, and most students who answered it just wrote "odds" or "probability" with no explanation. My most ambitious students did have an explanation—something like, "I would prefer to know the odds because I like odds better." My expectations were not met, but it was my fault for not giving my students the learning structures to meet my expectations.

Learning structures for critical thinking are no different than learning structures for grammar or basic math facts. They can and must be taught, as they are a crucial prerequisite for implementing thinkLaw strategies in your classroom. Band teachers almost always teach beginner students clapping exercises so they can master rhythm and timing before they even start to play their instruments. Think of learning structures as giving our students that rhythm. If we can get them to hold a beat, we can make this work even if they play off-key!

To ensure that you have the necessary tools to implement thinkLaw strategies for all of the students you serve, this section outlines the four most important structures for critical thinking you can seamlessly integrate into your instruction: Wait Time, Sentence Frames, Fishbowls, and Norms for Civil Discourse.

# Wait Time

Why might today's students struggle with critical thinking more than students in the past? Reading this question likely brings you immediately into "kids these days with their rock and roll" mode. Technology breeds instant gratification, and it's easy to see kids texting and chatting each other all day without any real interactions. But suppose I asked the question differently. Take a look at this question, and follow my instructions:

I want to ask you an important question, and I want you to really think about the answer. I am going to give you ten seconds to think. Why might today's students struggle with critical thinking more than students in the past? Think about your response silently for ten seconds.

Does this feel different, awkward, or unnatural? Time is of the essence when your job requires you to provide 180 days of learning in time for standardized exams that occur around 140 days in—and that is without accounting for those lovely picture days, holiday concerts, fire drills, spirit weeks, and everything else that sucks away time. This sense of urgency often results in teachers overlooking a powerful, free resource that is arguably the most important prerequisite for students to have access to critical thinking: wait time.

Albert Einstein once said, "If I had an hour to solve a problem, I'd spend 55 minutes thinking about the problem and 5 minutes thinking about solutions." It is literally impossible for students to think critically if we do not give them the time to do so, making wait time one of the most precious resources for learning.

There is a three-step process for executing wait time effectively:

1. Tell students, "I am going to give you ten seconds to think about your answer to this question."
2. Ask a thought-provoking, open-ended question.
3. Explicitly tell students, "Think about your response silently for ten seconds."

If you want to up the ante further, immediately after the ten second period elapses, ask students to do a short "turn and talk" to share their response briefly with the person right next to them. Talking is thinking out loud, so this is another way to give students more opportunities to engage in critical thinking.

Wait time is a powerful strategy for leveling the playing field. When you use wait time, you create more equitable opportunities for students to meaningfully contribute. All students benefit from wait time: those who struggle to find the right words, slower processers, super thoughtful learners, and even those students who always have an answer ready to go, whether that answer is asinine or not.

As a critical thinking disposition, wait time is an essential habit. Students must learn to value reflection over perfection. Society idolizes *Jeopardy!* champions who show how amazing they are at answering random questions in less than five seconds. But imagine your students growing up. Think about what the world would look like if, at the moment they recognize a challenging decision in front of them, their first instinct is to stop and think: *Should I make this huge purchase I can't really afford? Should I sign this contract right away? I'm short on cash, but I have the opportunity to take out this payday loan—should I do it?* Wait time builds the muscle memory necessary to approach life's important decisions with thoughtfulness by default.

This thoughtfulness is more important than ever in the current era of "no takebacks" on social media. Stories, Snapchat, and other ephemeral messages "disappear" but never truly disappear. Tweets or other social media posts, even if deleted, can be screenshotted or otherwise captured for permanent use. Either way, words matter. Reactions matter. Text messages sent cannot be unsent. This is one of those strategies that is just as important for helping our students push through challenging critical thinking problems in academics as it is for helping them process similar tough decisions in life.

## Sentence Frames

When educators want to set up students to write to a high level of expectations, they typically provide them with a rubric. They might even show them a sample of what "good" writing looks like. But giving students the structure to actually reach these expectations is an entirely different challenge. In law school, the standard legal writing model is IRAC (Issue, Rule, Analysis, Conclusion). Schools across the country often use a model similar to C-E-R (Claim, Evidence, Reasoning) or E & E (Evidence and Elaboration). But analysis, reasoning, and elaboration are the areas where student writing often falls apart despite students having a rubric. DRAAW+C helps students to navigate the high-level aspects of the analysis piece; applying sentence frames to this framework provides a clear template for helping students gain muscle memory for the nuts and bolts of analysis.

Let's use a controversial question to try out this structure: *Should college athletes be paid? Why or why not? Explain.*

Going back to the DRAAW+C framework, we want students to have a clear Decision, supported by an underlying Rule, Arguments on at least two sides, a "what would the World look like" public policy consequence argument, and a Conclusion. Knowing this, we might set up sentence frames like this:

**D:** College athletes <u>should/should not</u> (circle one) be paid.

**R:** College athletes _____ (explain the rule currently defining how college athletes are legally allowed to receive benefits for playing).

**A:** College athletes _____ (use the response in your decision) be paid because _____ (provide a persuasive reason supporting your decision).

**A:** On the other hand, some might argue that college athletes _____ (use the opposite response to your decision) be paid because _____ (provide a persuasive reason supporting the opposing side).

**W:** If student athletes _____ (use the decision you did not select), this would lead to _____ (explain a potential negative consequence).

**C:** Therefore, student athletes _____ (repeat your decision) get paid.

Applying this structure to the gambling example posed earlier in this chapter (would it be better for a gambler to know the probability or odds of an event occurring?) would look like this:

**D:** If I was a gambler, I would prefer to know the _____ (odds or probability) of an event occurring.

**R:** You determine odds of an event happening by _____ _____. The probability of an event happening is determined by _____ _____.

**A:** As a gambler, I would prefer to know the _____ of an event happening because _____ (provide a reason why knowing this value might be easier or more useful).

**A:** Others might prefer to know the _____ of an event happening because _____ (provide a reason why some might find the other value easier or more useful).

**W:** If gamblers had to use the _____ (the one you did not select) of an event happening instead of the _____, it would lead to _____ (explain a negative potential consequence).

**C:** Therefore, if I was a gambler, I would prefer to know the _____ (repeat your decision) of an event happening.

There are some important considerations to keep in mind when using sentence frames:

**Not all students need sentence frames.** Use these as a guide to turn your rubric into actionable steps for students to follow to meet your expectations. But feel free to have advanced learners approach these tasks without sentence frames at all or wean them off of sentence frames quickly. You can also feel free to have less-structured and more-structured sentence frames as a differentiation strategy.

**Sentence frames can and should be phased out.** As part of encouraging a gradual release of responsibility, you could consider sentence frames only when you are introducing a new type of writing prompt. Phasing these out over time ensures that students do not become too dependent on these frameworks.

**Sentence frames have broad applications.** I used two examples of how you can create sentence frames for a DRAAW+C analysis. But sentence frames can be used to model expectations for all sorts of tasks:

- **Test corrections:** I got this problem wrong because I _____ (explain your error). To fix this, I _____ (explain how you corrected it).

- **Evidence-based analysis:** On page _____ (provide the page number of what you are citing), the author argues that _____ (explain argument). This supports _____ (repeat your claim) because _____ (explain why this evidence supports your claim).

- **Compare and contrast:** _____ (item one) and _____ (item two) are alike because _____ (explain what they have in common).

# Fishbowls and Rubrics for Group Work

Placing students in small groups is often the default tactic for engagement. However, it is often a crapshoot as to whether any actual learning is happening in these groups. As educators, we intuitively understand what effective group work looks like and sounds like. But why do we assume students know this? Group work is another opportunity to provide students with explicit frameworks.

Instead of leaving the definition of effective group work open to interpretation, define it. Figure 12.1 is a simple rubric to evaluate the effectiveness of group work based on the categories of Participation, Time Management, and Better Together.

Note that this rubric does not punish off-task behavior. It is okay for students to laugh in groups, socialize, and go on random tangents here and there. What really matters is that every group member meaningfully participates. This does not mean that one person was the scribe, one was the timekeeper, and one was the presenter. It means that all group members are either providing helpful ideas or asking helpful questions.

Time should also be managed effectively. This means that group members thoroughly complete every part of the group task. Effective time management involves many other skills and strategies, especially in groups. But the expectation that groups will complete every task thoroughly sets the standard high and heightens focus on completing the task within the given time constraints.

Lastly, the group has to be greater than its individual parts. Better Together is a timely metric for 21st-century learning. When group members incorporate alternative viewpoints and questions raised into their answers, they are effectively speaking to be understood and listening to understand. Students are adopting the crucial habit of learning how to disagree without being disagreeable.

Whether you are just starting to use groups in your classes or you want to reboot what you have been doing, try using a fishbowl to model effective group work. Give your entire classroom the effective group work

**FIGURE 12.1**
*Group Work Rubric*

|  | 1 | 2 | 3 |
|---|---|---|---|
| **Participation** | One or more group members did not contribute any ideas or questions to the group. | Every group member contributed ideas or questions, but participation from one or more group members was minimal and/or unhelpful. | All group members either asked several helpful questions or provided several helpful ideas. |
| **Time Management** | The group was not able to complete one or more important parts of the group task. | The group technically completed every part of the group task, but spent only minimal time on one or more important parts of it. | The group thoroughly completed every part of the group task. |
| **Better Together** | The group completed the task without anyone questioning the outcome or providing alternate viewpoints. | One or more group members seriously questioned the outcome or provided serious alternate viewpoints, but these questions and viewpoints were not incorporated into the final product. | One or more group members questioned the outcome or provided alternate viewpoints that were incorporated into the final product. |

rubric (see Figure 12.1) and have one group complete a short five minute model task in front of the entire class. Then have the entire class, including the group itself, evaluate the fishbowl group. Ask the group to share its self-evaluation first, and then ask the rest of the class to share evaluations. As students share why and how they scored the group's effectiveness the way they did, they will become more intimately familiar with the expectations that will help them succeed in your classroom and in life.

# Norms for Civil Discourse

When students hear the word *debate*, what are they typically expecting? The same thing they see on cable news programs and sports channels, in barbershops and hair salons, and at family dinners on the holidays: arguing, arguing, and more arguing. To create safe, thoughtful spaces for students to freely explore the various critical thinking strategies provided in this book, norms for civil discourse may be helpful. Whether students are analyzing sensitive issues regarding free speech in schools or determining whether there is anything inherently bad about the Big Bad Wolf, discussions can get out of hand without clear guidelines.

Figure 12.2 contains five norms you can share with your students. Alter or add to this list as necessary.

Without a practical set of norms, students will have difficulty developing the habit of listening to understand and speaking to be understood. Traits like being able to disagree without being disagreeable must be taught, modeled, and mastered just like academic content.

There is probably an entire book to be written on helpful strategies teachers can use to explicitly scaffold instruction to maximize the impact of thinkLaw critical thinking strategies. But, like a band teacher laying the foundation for music with rhythm, the scaffolds for critical thinking laid out in this chapter provide students with the foundation to grow the critical thinking skills and dispositions they need.

**FIGURE 12.2**

*Norms for Civil Discourse*

| Norm | Rationale |
|---|---|
| Criticize the idea, not the person. | Students should be able to disagree with each other's ideas without demonizing those they disagree with. When a culture develops around critiquing ideas instead of people, it helps students feel safer and more likely to be open-minded about changing their minds. |
| Use "I" statements (when talking about an idea, say "I think" or "I disagree" rather than "people think," "we think," or "you think"). | Saying "I don't agree with Colin's argument that student athletes should be paid" sounds and feels much better than saying "Colin's argument that student athletes should be paid is not right." Even though you are singling out my argument, and not me personally, omitting the "I" makes this a much more declarative statement, putting me in defense – much less likely to listen to your reasoning. |
| Do not interrupt. | If you constantly interrupt, this is a clear indication that you have little to no interest in listening. When you care so much about making your next point that you do not allow others to complete theirs, the environment becomes far less civil. |
| Agree to disagree. | It is okay not to agree. In fact, it is a tremendous sign of intellectual maturity to disagree without being disagreeable. |
| Listen, even if you disagree. | Disagreements are normal. It is rare, however, to disagree with others but have the emotional intelligence to under-stand why they see an issue differently than you do. Understanding starts by listening. An environment where students speak to be understood and listen to understand is primed to be far more civil. |

# Chapter 13

# Avoiding Engagement for Engagement's Sake

"Students just are not engaged" is the lament of many frustrated administrators and teachers. When we picture what good teaching looks like, we think about students at the edge of their seats, yearning for learning, participating, working in groups, breaking a sweat, laughing, and having obnoxiously loud "aha" moments—the whole shebang. We have all heard the mantra that no student is ever going to come home and tell their parents, "Wow, we did an amazing worksheet today." It is no wonder that we tend to place such a premium on student engagement.

My purpose in this chapter, however, is not to be anti-student engagement. It is to ensure that we are using engagement for the sake of learning instead of for engagement's sake. The following example illuminates why this distinction is so important.

Meyer Levin, or I.S. 285, as the New York City Department of Education likes to call it, was the absolute best educational experience of my life. Maybe I was a weirdo, but I thought middle school was the greatest time a kid could ever dream of. My sixth grade math teacher excited me so much about math that I was the proudest member of the math team in this Brooklyn, NY, school. So, when I decided to be a math teacher myself and had some time to observe teachers after college graduation, I visited Ms. Williams, who was now the math department chair.

DOI: 10.4324/9781003482147-17

I told her of my big plans to bring tons of fun, joy, and excitement into the math classroom and the amazing project-based learning themes I had been thinking up. But before I went further and shared a preview of my acceptance speech for Rookie Teacher of the Year, she stopped me and said, "Come with me so I can show you something." (When your middle school teacher tells you to do something, even as an adult, you basically just have to do it.)

Ms. Williams wanted to teach me the most important lesson that she thought I needed to know: student engagement does not equal student learning. True, students need to be engaged to some extent to learn, but engagement for engagement's sake doesn't necessarily translate to meaningful learning opportunities. I had no idea what she was talking about until she and I observed two math teachers who taught the same grade level and who were both teaching a lesson on averages that day.

Teacher A was every student's favorite teacher. Her class was lively, full of energy, and had lots of group work and student participation. The exhilarating mood of her classroom was so palpable that I could imagine she was a principal's dream. But despite all of her classroom's bells and whistles, a lot of the student responses I observed in group work were incorrect. Even though several of these students, who knew I was observing as a newly minted teacher, told me as they exited that I should teach just like Teacher A, ultimately her students left class without a true understanding of the lesson's objective: calculating averages.

Teacher B's classroom was far different. She had a more reserved energy, and there was no "wow" factor. She opened class with a story about watching a *60 Minutes* episode in which a reporter interviewed a South African leader during the apartheid era. At first, even I was thinking, "This is 2004 in East Flatbush... why is she sharing this irrelevant story?" But she went on to explain that when the reporter asked a question about South Africa's incredible income gap, the government official defensively responded by explaining that the average South African income was one of the highest in the world. The interviewer's follow-up question left the official speechless, and when Teacher B shared it with the class, it caused a metaphysical change in every student in that classroom: "If one of your feet is in a bucket of boiling water, and your other foot is in bucket of ice cold water, on average, are you comfortable?"

Like a bucket of cold water, a realization washed over me: the best teachers aren't just engaging but also purposeful in where that engagement leads. In my work with thinkLaw, I've gained an ever deeper understanding of the undeniable fact that *engagement is not the same as student learning.*

Engaging and purposeful lesson planning go hand in hand. Without both we can't get our students to achieve the objectives of the day. Teacher B's engagement worked because it sparked intrinsic motivation. Students were intrigued to learn more about averages because she couched her lesson around a core issue of fairness and justice. Her students developed a more intuitive understanding of averages because of her bucket analogy, allowing them to estimate the answers to their average problems before performing the average formula.

When we think about designing lessons to engage our students, we must remember that is only half the battle. To help students unleash their full potential, we must combine the type of engagement that taps into our students' sense of agency with a purposeful focus on learning outcomes.

# Chapter 14

# Critical Thinking

*Classroom Management's Secret Weapon*

thinkLaw strategies work extremely well in a courtroom. It probably helps that no one is allowed to talk, every person in the courtroom is required to treat the judge with extreme deference, and anyone who is not complying with the court's rules can be held in contempt and taken out of court in handcuffs. However, real classrooms do not and should not work this way.

Incorporating critical thinking into your class daily is extremely challenging when you are dealing with extremely challenging behaviors simultaneously. Every educator has "that" student—the brilliant born leader, innovator, and amazing problem-solver who also happens to be a frequent flier in disciplinary referrals, detentions, and visits to the principal's office. But considering the type of teacher-driven, content-heavy instruction that students are typically getting (especially during testing season), it should be no surprise that bright and high-energy students sometimes struggle with behavioral issues and pose challenges to effective classroom management. So, here are three powerful but practical strategies that leverage critical thinking instruction as a proactive classroom management tool for some of the most common disruptive student behaviors.

DOI: 10.4324/9781003482147-18

# Talking: Don't Fight It, Invite It

Excessive, off-task student talking is probably the most common disruption for a meaningful learning environment. Instead of giving out teacher stares, saying the painful "I'll wait" phrase (I promised I would never use that phrase as an educator, but it's hard not to sometimes), or otherwise punishing students for the natural inclination to want to talk, build multiple opportunities for students to engage in compelling conversations in your classroom.

Almost every student responds to issues around fairness and justice or learning activities involving debate because they are craving opportunities to use their voices. So why not design talk-heavy learning activities? In science, students might review and debate viewpoints on evolution and whether the earth is round. In math, they might take the opportunity to look at two incorrect problems and argue over which should receive more credit. Don't fight the talking; invite it!

# Get Moving

Another strategy to proactively address classroom management is combining movement and critical thinking. Schools have come a long way in recognizing that movement is important to student learning, but many teachers still struggle when students frequently get out of their seats or otherwise physically disrupt the classroom environment. Intentionally building movement into your lessons proactively addresses this challenge. Conduct polls and have students move around the room based on their viewpoints. Allow students to move back and forth if they end up changing their minds. Use fun dance videos to help students memorize vocabulary words in geometry. When you just can't avoid long blocks of delivering nothing but content, a good old-fashioned stretch session is another way to get those juices flowing in your students.

# Building a Positive Classroom Culture through Empathy

Bullying and other antisocial behaviors are probably some of the most serious threats to a safe and productive learning environment faced by teachers. So many powerful antibullying and social-emotional learning programs have done a great job in addressing these challenges, but teachers have the power to tackle these issues within their own instruction. Every state has some English language arts standard for every grade level about speaking, listening, and asking questions to understand a speaker's purpose and perspective. Even the Next Generation Science Standards call for students to be able to look at arguments from multiple perspectives and to respectfully give and receive critiques through a back-and-forth process.

Designing lessons with questions that do not have a clear right or wrong answer—especially questions that involve a "what would you do if this were you" component—is a meaningful way to build empathy by encouraging students to put themselves in another person's shoes and see different perspectives.

# Reframing Disruptors as Innovators

Deeper learning activities that involve engaging and rigorous critical thinking should be the first tool educators grab from their educational toolbox to improve classroom management. But this chapter is just a snippet of all of the instructional strategies you can use to reach "that" student.

We have a serious issue with the way we approach discipline in education. As much as we hear about the disparate consequences for students of color and the unintended (or maybe intended) consequences of zero-tolerance policies, my issue isn't about those injustices. My issue is about how educators can best serve the students I firmly believe are best equipped to be the leaders we need in the 21st century. If we do this right, the "bad" students of today can easily become the phenomenal leaders we need to lead us into the future.

I have attended more than 100 education conferences in the past three years. So, I hear a lot about leadership. Leaders go against the grain. They march to the beat of their own drum. They ask for forgiveness, not permission. They defy norms. They don't follow the rules; they change the game. In fact, we lionize the most innovative people in business and industry and call them "disruptors." Given that all of these descriptions also apply to "bad" students, we must accept that our disciplinary practices force us to leave potential greatness on the table for far too many.

To be clear, I understand fully that students cannot learn in a chaotic classroom where students are doing whatever they feel like with no structure and no consequences. This is not a call for schools to adopt the exact opposite of a zero-tolerance policy. But imagine a world where instead of thinking of students who always get into some sort of trouble as "bad," we see their leadership potential and own up to the necessary, albeit challenging, responsibility to help them fulfill this potential.

One of the keys to unleashing students' full potential for 21st-century leadership is tapping into their critical thinking. For example, in 2017, thinkLaw partnered with Miley Achievement Center, a Las Vegas, NV, school in the Clark County School District for students who typically cannot return to their schools for an extended period because of severe disciplinary infractions. On its face, this doesn't sound like a group of students who would normally be in a program that teaches critical thinking through real-life legal cases. Usually we expect this kind of instruction for the gifted and talented kids, the Advanced Placement classes, or the honors courses. But in reality, "bad" students—or "disruptors," as I call them—are particularly equipped to thrive when challenged with critical thinking. According to Gordon Stewart, Miley's assistant principal, thinkLaw's lessons "engaged students in critical thinking exceptionally well, especially because so many of our students already spend so much time thinking about gray areas." (personal communication, September 11, 2018). In other words, when we create classroom spaces for learning where talking is encouraged, motivation is intrinsic, and students bring their so-called "disruptive tendencies" to the table as an asset in the learning process, we all win.

Part of why educators often struggle to reframe disruptors with a positive framing is explained by the common answer educators give to this question: would you describe yourself as a "good" student or a "bad" student? I've asked thousands of educators this question during critical thinking workshops I've delivered across the country. More than 80% of educators labeled themselves as "good" rule-followers who rarely got in trouble. Growing up, I was in the other 20%. But I was lucky because at a very young age, a teacher's aide saw past my nonsense and asked my mom to get me tested for entry into the gifted and talented program in another district. When I got in, the craziest thing happened: the same behaviors I would get in trouble for—talking, arguing, getting out of my seat, laughing too hard (yup, that was a thing), and asking "smart aleck" questions (that was a thing, too)—were rewarded in my gifted class. In fact, my class was always pretty loud and chaotic, probably because the teacher at the front of the class presumed that every single student was capable of learning and being challenged with rigorous and engaging content. Don't let your bias determine how you view "disruptors" in your class. Instead, ensure that you seek out strategies to unleash the unlimited potential of these natural leaders and not just rein them in.

# Chapter 15

# Beyond Test Prep

*Hacking the "Big Test"*

"I've got some amazing project-based learning ideas that will light a fire under my students. I can't wait to do them... after testing!" If this sounds familiar, then you have firsthand experience with the pressure to cover ungodly amounts of material before high-stakes exams. Too often, this pressure creates a joyless experience for teachers and students alike. But what if it didn't have to be this way?

Some readers probably want to skip this chapter. Standardized tests have sucked all of the air out of the room in the current era of accountability. Amazing teachers feel like sellouts when they feel pressured to push aside what they know about good teaching so they can start the mindless process of teaching to the test. I get it. But I often wonder if we understand the equity issues at stake when it comes to testing.

When I say equity and testing, I am not referring to the mountains of evidence suggesting that tests are culturally biased, nor the results that show that low-income and minority students disproportionately do poorly on these exams. Instead, I am referring to equity of outcomes. If we truly believe that education ought to transform opportunities for children by breaking cycles of poverty, we must also believe that doing well on exams matters. Lawyers have to take the LSAT and pass the bar. Doctors have to take the MCAT, the USMLE, and Board exams. Engineers, nurses, and numerous other professions still use tests as barriers for access.

DOI: 10.4324/9781003482147-19

Whether these barriers are fair is not my concern. My concern is that we should not live in a world where only the students who can afford expensive test prep programs have access to the practical strategies they need to succeed on these exams. We owe it to our students to teach them how to be successful on the various types of tests they will face academically, professionally, and in life. Giving students the tools and strategies they need to conquer these exams does not mean that educators need to compromise good teaching.

What if you could engage students in rigorous and engaging learning activities and ensure they were prepared for exams that have become increasingly challenging over time? Hacking test prep with critical thinking is not only feasible, but also necessary, because let's be real: if there were such a thing as "teaching to the test," we would have cracked that code by now. Whether your state uses the PARCC, SBAC, STAAR, AzMERIT, SOL, or a different assessment, rote memorization and spoonfed learning are not going to prepare students for success on these exams. Here's an example of why drill-and-kill doesn't work:

> A sandwich shop offers a 15% discount when a customer spends at least $75. The shop sells sandwiches for $8.25 each and cookies for $1.45 each.
> Juliana buys 8 sandwiches.
> What is the least number of cookies that Juliana can buy and still get the discount?

This question, adapted from a real-life standardized exam, is a perfect example of why teaching to the test is impossible. To get this question right, a student needs to understand the purpose of five different numbers, avoid being fooled by the 15% figure (which is not relevant to the problem), understand how inequalities are set up, and know how to multiply decimals, subtract whole numbers, and divide decimals. If that isn't enough, the student must recognize that Juliana can't buy 6.2 cookies, so she will have to buy 7 in order to get the discount. Adding to the difficulty, this is a grid item response. In other words, this is not one of those multiple-choice questions where a student can guess or use process of elimination to solve.

As common as drill-and-kill worksheets and *Jeopardy!*-style review games are, these strategies simply will not cut it. Students need critical thinking to apply their knowledge and exercise tons of logical reasoning to work through tricky multistep and multiple-choice questions. The three strategies discussed in this chapter that you can use to "hack" test prep with critical thinking are Teaching to the Test Format, the WISE Method of problem solving, and Thinking Like Joe Schmo.

## Teaching to the Test Format

I have a dorky confession: I truly love taking standardized exams. Whenever I am getting ready to train teachers in a new state, one of my most exciting preparation activities is completing an elementary, middle, and high school practice state exam in math and English language arts. I love doing this because it helps me appreciate just how high the bar has been raised for our students when it comes to expectations for achievement. Growing up, my math exams were 100% multiple choice, mostly involving problems requiring basic computation. Today's math exams have complex open-ended responses, graphs, and easy-to-mess-up "select all of the answers that are correct" problems.

Growing up, my reading exams were cloze tests; they were literally fill-in-the-blank exams that asked students to figure out the right word to go into a sentence. That was it. There was no writing an essay after analyzing multiple different sources. There was no correcting sentences with improper usage of grammar. I was never asked to drag and drop lines from an essay that supported specific claims the author made. Succeeding on today's tests is as much about knowing the test format as it is knowing the test content.

Between the mechanics of tests that are increasingly computerized and the ever-evolving format of test questions, it often seems like these tests are measuring the ability to understand test logistics just as much as the questions themselves. With so many states struggling with teacher shortages, it is common for systems to recruit lots of teachers from other states, and even teachers from other countries. Asking teachers to prepare students to excel on exams with formats these teachers may be completely unfamiliar with is a recipe for disaster. Especially when our most transient students face a similar challenge.

There is a powerful case to be made, however, for the connection between mastering test formats and equipping students with the critical thinking they need to be prepared for the future of work. Considering the world we are preparing our students for, where they will need to solve problems we haven't identified yet using technologies that haven't been created yet in career fields that do not currently exist, there is inherent value in equipping our students with the adaptability needed to respond to questions in lots of unfamiliar formats. Learning how to learn is a core aspect of 21st-century readiness, so the choice between critical thinking and adherence to test questions is a false choice.

Teaching to the Test Format is not a February "it's time for test prep" problem. This is a problem educators should be addressing from the beginning of the year. There are three steps to Teaching to the Test Format.

1. Create a list of all of the different types of question formats used on the exam with concrete examples of each. Whether students are prepping for the SAT, ACT, AP exams, or statewide assessments, there are countless free resources that you can look up to help. These are often found on your state's website or on the website for the company that created the exam.

2. Make an honest assessment of what types of questions you prefer and what types of questions you dislike. My mother does not like eggs in her potato salad, so she never put eggs in her potato salad, and now I do not like eggs in my potato salad. If a certain type of question makes you feel the way my mother feels about eggs, be careful that you do not unintentionally fail to give students practice in question formats they need to be comfortable with.

3. Third, create a list divided into three categories: (1) question types you frequently use with your students, (2) question types you sometimes use with your students, and (3) question types you never use with your students. Once this list is created, you can start seamlessly integrating more of these question types into your instruction, practice, and assessments so students can become more comfortable answering questions in multiple formats. You will probably not be able to give your students significant amounts of practice for some question types that are specific to the computerized platform used to take the test. In these cases, you can still take the time to show students an example of how problems like these are solved by logging into one of the sample test portals so they have some idea of what to expect.

The key takeaway is this: we do not want to give our students the academic skills to master these exams, and then have them do poorly simply because they are providing the right answer in the wrong way.

# The WISE Method

There is *a lot* going on in the fifth grade problem in Figure 15.1.

This is a question where "guesstimating in complete sentences" can be a powerful tool. To get students set up with success and with a contextual understanding to help them make effective predictions and inferences for a reasonable answer, start with the ending. Students should highlight the question (What is the fewest number of cases of bottled water Greg will need to provide for all of the athletes, coaches, and judges at the track meet?) and prepare an answer like this:

---

**FIGURE 15.1**
*Fifth Grade Multistep Word Problem*

Greg is volunteering at a track meet. He is in charge of providing the bottled water. Greg knows these facts:

- The track meet will last 3 days.
- There will be 117 athletes, 7 coaches, and 4 judges attending the track meet.
- One case of bottled water contains 24 bottles.

The table shows the number of bottles of water each athlete, coach, and judge will get for each day of the track meet.

**Bottled Water for Track Meet**

| Person Attending | Number of Bottles |
|---|---|
| Athlete | 4 |
| Coach | 3 |
| Judge | 2 |

What is the **fewest** number of cases of bottled water Greg will need to provide for all the athletes, coaches, and judges at the track meet? Show your work or explain how you found your answer using equations.

_____ is the fewest number of cases of bottled water Greg will need to provide for all of the athletes, coaches, and judges at the track meet.

Because beginning with the end in mind is such a useful tool for problem solving, this is the basis for the WISE Method of problem solving: Write, Investigate, Setup, and Evaluate. This five-step process is outlined in Figure 15.2.

The WISE Method graphic organizer is designed to help students push through the psychological barrier of the open-ended response. The best way to get started on a problem is to get started on a problem. The WISE Method helps students get beyond a blank page by having them start by writing down (W) what the question is asking. Then, students will move diagonally to the evaluate box (E) to write using the guesstimating in complete sentences strategy with a blank answer.

Now, without doing much hard work or analysis, students are done with half of the WISE graphic organizer. The investigation box (I) simply asks students to list the important facts in a problem. I recommend having students use dashes to make their list instead of doing a numbered or lettered list to limit confusion. The investigation should be limited to only the pertinent facts of the problem. Students should also organize their information in a way that makes it easier to piece together the problem.

FIGURE 15.2
*WISE Method Graphic Organizer*

| **W**rite (1st step)<br>Rewrite what the question is actually asking. | **I**nvestigate (3rd step)<br>List <u>only</u> the important information in every problem. |
|---|---|
| **S**etup (4th step)<br>Explain setup and compute solution, showing all steps along the way. Be careful to note any special considerations. | **E**valuate (2nd and 5th step)<br>a) Write the blank answer in a complete sentence.<br>b) Fill in the blank and verify the answer to check its accuracy **(justification is usually in the setup).** |

For example, in this problem, students could write that there are 117 athletes, and then write in a separate line that each athlete drinks four bottles a day. But it might be more useful to organize these facts so that we can see in one line that each of the 117 athletes drinks four bottles a day. Most students will not have significant challenges with listing the facts of an investigation. As a result, by the time students complete the third part of the WISE Method, their graphic organizer is mostly complete, and they are a long way away from the blank response they started with. See Figure 15.3 for an example of a completed WISE organizer.

The setup (S) is likely the most challenging part of WISE Method. Here, students need to explain what they are planning on doing and then actually do it. Because of the power of metacognition, this process works best when you ask students to write a brief summary of their plan for solving

---

**FIGURE 15.3**
*Completed WISE Method Graphic Organizer*

| **W**rite (1st step) | **I**nvestigate (3rd step) |
|---|---|
| What is the **fewest** number of cases of bottled water Greg will need to provide for all the athletes, coaches, and judges at the track meet? | - 3-day track meet<br>- 117 athletes, and each drinks 4 bottles a day<br>- 7 coaches, and each drinks 3 bottles a day<br>- 4 judges, and each drinks 2 bottles a day<br>- Each case has 24 bottles |
| **S**etup (4th step) | **E**valuate (2nd and 5th step) |
| Need to figure out how much water all three groups of people drink each day, multiply that by three, and then divide the total amount by 24 to figure out how many cases. And if we are short some bottles, I need to make sure I add a whole additional case.<br><br>$(117*4) + (7*3) + (4*2) = 497$<br>$497*3 = 1491$<br>$1491/24 = 62.125$ (add another case) → 63 | ____ is the **fewest** number of cases of bottled water Greg will need to provide for all the athletes, coaches, and judges at the track meet. |

the problem. Allowing students to commit the voices in their head into writing helps them visualize their plan, account for any special considerations, and more clearly see potential holes in their reasoning.

Here, the basic setup might look like this: "Need to figure out how much water all three groups of people drink each day, multiply that by 3, and then divide that total amount by 24 to figure out how many cases." But when students take the additional step of accounting for any special considerations, they have to realize that unless the total number is a multiple of 24, they will probably have to order another case of water. Then, and only then, should students start the process of computing the problem. Carefully setting up a problem in the WISE Method also applies to writing essays, responding to science lab questions, or completing whatever task is being asked of students in whatever subject area is being assessed.

The final evaluation steps are to complete the blank and to check the final answer. The complete sentence should already be there, so the number 63 should be added. To evaluate and verify that this response is accurate, students can use an estimation strategy like rounding to ensure that their answer is in the right ballpark. If they round the number of athletes to 120 times 4 bottles each, they get 480. Seven coaches times 3 bottles each rounds to about 20. And 4 judges times 2 bottles per judge rounds to 10. This brings the estimated total to 510 bottles per day. That's about 500 times 3 days, which results in 1,500. If students divide by 25 (because who estimates using the number 24?), they know the answer should be somewhere in the neighborhood of 60, which is super close to the final answer of 63. Training students in the process of guesstimating in complete sentences helps them develop much more reasonable answers.

## Thinking Like Joe Schmo

In Chapter 8, while discussing the thinkLaw framework of Mistake Analysis, I introduced Joe Schmo, the student who always falls for the trick answer, does not read the directions carefully, or fails to complete all of the steps in a problem. Developing a healthy sense of skepticism is a powerful component of critical thinking. Take a look at the fifth-grade problem shared in Figure 15.4 to see why this trait is so important. Teaching students to Think Like Joe Schmo can help them avoid making mistakes due to a common technique used by test makers.

---

**FIGURE 15.4**

*Thinking Like Joe Schmo Sample Problem*

For a family gathering, Brittany made 5 meat loafs using 9 pounds of ground beef. She also made 14 hamburgers using 4 pounds of ground beef.

**Part A**

Each meat loaf was made with the same amount of ground beef.
Which of these is closest to the amount of ground beef in each meat loaf?

- ○ A. ½ pound
- ○ B. 1 pound
- ○ C. 1 ½ pounds
- ○ D. 2 pounds

---

As a former "I must be the first kid done" student, I initially rushed through this problem. I saw that the problem was asking about meat loaf and ground beef, saw 5 meat loaves, 9 pounds, and thought, "Easy! That's just 5/9, which is about 1/2." Then, I realized that was choice A. I then asked myself, "Are you about to fall for the Choice A gotcha? Nope!"

The question asked how many pounds of ground beef were used for each meat loaf. This means I should have taken the 9 and divided by 5, giving me 9/5, which is close to 2, not 1/2. It is not a coincidence that in this problem, the number 5 appears before the number 9. We read numbers from left to right, and if you read this problem without paying close attention to what the question is really asking, you fall right into the Choice A gotcha.

Although this problem was straightforward, test makers often design questions that require students to look at a variety of answer choices with a trick answer for Choice A, specifically targeting fast test takers like myself. When students realize the way these tests try to fool you, they can't help but to develop skepticism about the test takers that try to catch them slipping. Students have to know how to think like Joe Schmo so they can avoid becoming him.

## Test Prep Can Be Awesome

After reviewing these strategies, I hope you agree that test prep does not have to be dreadful. Fully preparing students for these tests with strategies like those presented in this chapter is as much about psychological preparedness as it is about academic preparedness. Test anxiety is a real challenge for so many of our students. When I worked with middle school students who struggled with less severe forms of test anxiety, I gave them a "test" with one question: "What's 1 + 1?" They laughed, wrote "2," and handed the test back to me. Why did they laugh? They explained that this is not how their test anxiety worked. They got anxious when the tests were high-stakes, challenging, long, strenuous, and confusing. They got anxious when they thought they knew something but then did not recognize the way the question was asked on the test.

So, for students who struggle with a moderate level of text anxiety (educators should speak to the families of students who struggle severely about seeking professional support), these Beyond Test Prep strategies are even more powerful. Imagine if students were as prepared for the various question formats and the twists and turns in exam questions as they were to answer "What's 1 + 1?" The confidence of knowing they can answer correctly because they have had explicit instruction and extensive practice is not just a test prep tool. This confidence is a crucial critical thinking disposition that will help our students work through challenging problems well beyond their end-of-year exams.

# Chapter 16

# Leveraging Families to Unleash Critical Thinking Potential

This chapter breaks down how and why parents and families must recognize, value, and leverage their power to support critical thinking development in their children. I was reminded of the importance of leveraging families during a conversation I had with my nephew when he spent a week in the summer with me before sixth grade. One day, he decided he wanted brownies. That sounded great, so we walked into the doors of the supermarket. But before we did anything, we made our game plan:

> **Me:** What do we need?
>
> **My nephew:** Brownies.
>
> **Me:** Anything else?
>
> **My nephew:** Oh, we should get milk, too.
>
> **Me:** Sounds delicious. Where do you think the milk is?
>
> **My nephew:** Probably in the back somewhere.
>
> **Me:** (In my most dramatic voice possible) Wait a minute! In the back? *Everyone* comes to the supermarket for milk. Why in the world would they put it in the back of the supermarket?

DOI: 10.4324/9781003482147-20

**My nephew:** I don't know, Uncle Colin.

**Me:** Look, I know you don't "know" know, but why do you *think* the milk is the back of the supermarket?

**My nephew:** Uncle Colin, if you know the answer, just tell me. I don't even want milk anymore.

This exchange stood out to me because as a child, I was the designated grocery shopping assistant as early as I can remember. I thought about all of the ways my mother made a dollar out of 15 cents through savvy coupon-clipping and finding sales. I thought about the nonstop thinking my mom did about what was about to run out at home, what fruits were in season, and whether or not a bulk purchase was actually a good deal.

I even thought beyond the supermarket. I made my own breakfast as soon as I could reach everything I needed for breakfast. Eggshells did not taste very good, so I learned how to break open eggs so I could have the non-crunchy version. I cooked entire meals by middle school, which mostly involved me learning how to salvage food after overseasoning and/or overcooking it. These experiences all added up to one thing: frequent opportunities for me to engage in productive struggle.

Why is the milk in the back of the supermarket? Maybe the store's owners want you to go through the entire store, buy a bunch of things you do not need, and end up forgetting the milk! Maybe the refrigerator section is in the back of the store, and when the dairy truck parks there, for the sake of food safety, it's easier to move milk straight into the refrigerator instead of carting the milk to the front of the store. But the milk is not the issue. The issue is that my nephew was not willing to engage in the productive struggle involved in answering this question.

But this does not have to be the case. The vast majority of parents regularly apply 21st-century skills in their day-to-day management of the household, even if they don't have a high school diploma and even if they do not speak English fluently. When schools are intentional about supporting parents in creating a culture of inquiry at home, those habits and mindsets transfer to the classroom.

A very wise kindergarten teacher, Mary Tierney, called me out at the end of one of my thinkLaw workshops and reminded me that I was missing a huge piece of the puzzle: parents and families have tremendous capacity to encourage critical thinking skills and dispositions at home through basic involvement in household tasks. There are four guiding principles I call ECHO strategies to help students through this:

1. Encouraging productive struggle,
2. Combating learned helplessness,
3. Helping without being too helpful, and
4. Objecting for no reason.

To ensure that these strategies actually reach our students' families, this chapter closes with practical tips to help families access these strategies.

# Encouraging Productive Struggle

Sloths are the slowest mammals in the world. But they are Formula One racecars compared to the way young people move in the morning when parents try to get them out of the house! With the pace of life moving so quickly, the default response to help children when they are struggling—tying shoes, getting dressed, cleaning up—is natural. But helping is also dangerous when it comes to building essential critical thinking dispositions in children.

As an example, my daughter loves pouring an ungodly amount of syrup on her pancakes. One morning at brunch, she tried to pour the syrup using her left hand, and it did not work. She made a confused face and tried to do it with her right hand, to no avail. I looked at her, saw her head spinning, and started rooting for her. "You got this, baby!" I said. I knew she would figure out that the bottle needed to be turned completely upside down for syrup to come out.

But before my baby girl could experience her victory, her sweet Nana said, "Come here, baby, let me help you." I dramatically yelled, "Nooooo," causing lots of awkward glares from the waitstaff and patrons of this restaurant. Perhaps I overreacted. But my overdramatic reaction came from understanding that this moment is where "it" starts—this destructive force of learned helplessness. I understood that the urge to help came from a place of love, but it denied my child the glory of productive struggle.

If "learning how to learn" is an essential critical thinking disposition, we need to create the space and time for children to figure problems out on their own. When children figure out the proper milk-to-cereal ratio themselves, that intrinsic joy of achieving a small miracle creates a foundation for continuous wonder and discovery, as well as the pride of accomplishing a task independently. Encourage parents to give their children a chance. Children might fail. But when they fail on their own, that is a successful step in the process of developing the independence and resilience life demands.

# Combating Learned Helplessness

Despite parents' best efforts, children may still develop habits of learned helplessness. There is no mistaking learned helplessness. When children say, "I can't do it," or ask for help before they have even tried to "do it" themselves, that is learned helplessness loud and clear. Fortunately, there are two strategies parents can use to combat this: (1) limiting lifesavers and (2) seeking specificity.

# Limiting Lifesavers

In real life, parents will never let children drown. But when it comes to children solving ordinary problems on their own, there is typically no life-or-death risk involved in forcing them to figure out how to stay afloat. Limiting lifesavers means that parents make it clear that the problem children are stuck on is a no-bailout situation. They are on their own unless and until they make a true attempt to solve their problem.

Tell students: don't understand a math problem? Take your best stab at it, show your work, and *then* I will look at it. But you must start it on your own. Left your homework at school? Figure out a plan to ensure you can have it turned in by tomorrow morning. Drowning in a pool? I'm going to jump in and save you immediately. Drowning in disorganization, missed assignments, or lost notes? I will not be your lifesaver. You need to research how to improve your organization systems. How do you spell _____ (pick a word, any word)? How do you spell "dictionary?"

# Seeking Specificity

This strategy comes in handy when children have made legitimate attempts to solve a problem but are still stuck. This technique still puts the power in children's hands by forcing them to explain why and how they are stuck, which often gives them ideas of how to fix the problem on their own. For parents, seeking specificity might sound something like this:

> **Me:** Put on your shirt, please.
>
> **My son:** I can't.
>
> **Me:** Why can't you put on your shirt?
>
> **My son:** Because it hurts.
>
> **Me:** Why does it hurt?
>
> **My son:** It hurts my head.
>
> **Me:** Show me how it hurts your head. (As my son puts on his shirt by sticking his arm through the hole for his head and starts trying to squeeze his head through one of the holes for the arm, he yells at me from under the hole that is entirely too big for his head.)
>
> **My son:** See, daddy! (I help him take the shirt off.)
>
> **Me:** Why was your head hurting you?
>
> **My son:** Because the hole was too small.
>
> **Me:** Which hole was too small?
>
> **My son:** (He figures it out.) Oh, I know how to do it!

Now, I understand that these situations do not always go so smoothly. But the basic idea of seeking specificity is that parents need children to clearly explain the problem they are trying to solve—the more specific, the better. There is very little anyone can do with "I don't understand" or "I can't." But when children develop clarity of what they do not understand and what they cannot do, they simultaneously learn what they need to understand and what they need to learn how to do. When children develop this level of clarity, it equips them with a strong foundation for "learning how to learn" in the school context, a fundamental component of a child's critical thinking toolset.

## Helping Without Being Too Helpful

When parents must help, they must avoid being too helpful. For example, if I am helping my child with math homework, he might have the following question:

> Juliana had 8 pairs of socks in her drawer. She took out 3 pairs of socks to pack for vacation. What fraction represents the number of pairs of socks Juliana did not take on vacation?

My son's answer: 3/8. The mistake here is clear. Instead of using the fraction Juliana did *not* take, he used the fraction representing what she *did* take. The right answer should be 5/8. The natural instinct with a mistake like this is for a parent to play the "good teacher" and explain this error fully to the child. Let's say a child got this question wrong on a test and was doing corrections at home. The "good teacher" conversation sounds something like this:

> **My son:** Why did I get this wrong?
>
> **Me:** Let me take a look. Oh, it's because instead of using the fraction Juliana did *not* take, you used the fraction representing what she *did* take. How many pairs of socks are there in total?
>
> **My son:** Eight pairs.
>
> **Me:** Yes. You got that part right. And how many pairs of socks did she take?
>
> **My son:** Three pairs.
>
> **Me:** Now what does the question say?
>
> **My son:** How much did she *not* take? Oh, the answer should be 5/8.

**Me:** Yes! Great job!

On the surface, this exchange seems perfectly harmless and entirely normal. But consider this alternative:

**My son:** Why did I get this wrong?

**Me:** Why do you think you got this wrong?

**My son:** I don't know. That's why I'm asking you.

**Me:** Read the question again, carefully. Look at your answer again. Then explain why you think you got it wrong.

Do you see a difference? In this second conversation, I immediately asked my son to do the heavy lifting instead of doing it for him. When he resisted, I gave him a general instruction that, again, forced him to take responsibility for figuring this problem out. Given that he clearly understands the concept of fractions and likely just did not read the question closely to see the "not," he will probably have his own "aha" moment at that point.

Because some children will just spin their wheels without more specific guidance, using the strategy of asking them to explain themselves may be helpful. So, here is another option that applies this practice:

**My son:** Why did I get this wrong?

**Me:** Explain to me how you got your answer.

**My son:** I read that she had eight pairs of socks in total and she took out three pairs for vacation. So, I made the fraction 3/8.

**Me:** Read the question again, carefully. Look at your answer again. Then explain why you think you got it wrong.

**My son:** Oh… how much did she *not* take. I figured it out.

The idea of helping without being too helpful applies to the example of my mother-in-law pouring the syrup for my daughter. If she wanted to help my daughter without being too helpful, she could have asked, "Why do you think the syrup isn't coming out?" Maybe my daughter would have said it was too thick. Maybe she would have tried to hit the jackpot by undoing the syrup dispenser altogether. But the solution would have been hers.

So, when parents want or need to help, they should offer the minimal amount of help necessary to ensure that the solution still belongs to their child. General instructions typically work very effectively in this context. For example: if a child's question is "How do I spell _____?", parents can tell the child, "Sound it out and see what it looks like." If a child still has to do the heavy lifting, there is a good chance that an adult's help is not too helpful.

Helping without being too helpful is a practical way to maximize the opportunities for children to work independently. If children can do a task themselves, parents should have them do it. If children can do a task with instruction, parents can ask a sibling or friend to help instead. Even if parents end up having to complete the task because their child cannot help, having the child watch encourages at least some level of involvement. Life is likely never going to fit into such neat categories, but parents are much more likely to foster independence in their children if they are intentional about it.

# Objecting for No Reason

"I object" may have been the reason I wanted to be a lawyer. Nothing is more exhilarating than seeing the dramatic objections made on television law shows and movies. Objections are less frequent and considerably less dramatic in real-life courtrooms. But objecting for no reason is a powerful tool for building critical thinking dispositions at home.

When I say objecting for no reason, I am referring to the practice of disagreeing with children for no other reason than to get them to develop claims and evidence to support their side. This is one of the more obnoxious options listed in this book, but a viable strategy, nonetheless. Here is what this might sound like:

> **Child:** 4 plus 3 is 7.
>
> **Parent:** That's not true. 4 plus 3 is 43.
>
> **Child:** No, it's not.

**Parent:** Yes, it is, because when you take a 4 and add a 3 to it, you get 43.

**Child:** No, that's not how you add! You are supposed to start with 4, count off three numbers—5, 6, 7—and you end up on 7, so the answer is 7.

**Parent:** Oh, right, right, right... thanks for the reminder.

This does not even have to always happen in an academic setting. Recently, I had the following conversation with my daughter after watching *The Lion King*:

**Me:** Who was the bad guy in that movie?

**My daughter:** Scar was the bad guy. He was really bad!

**Me:** No, you are so wrong. Mufasa was bad. And Simba was the absolute worst!

**My daughter:** What? Scar killed Mufasa, and he and the hyenas were messing up Pride Rock.

**Me:** Mufasa was basically bullying the hyenas, and he gave Scar a scar for life in a fight that happened before the movie. He pushed Scar out to the edge of Pride Rock. And Simba—don't get me started on Simba.

To ensure that you do not think less of me as a human being, I want to clarify that I do think Scar is very, very bad. But I also think objecting to ideas like this is a very good way to push children to think beyond the surface. In objection mode, the goal is to play devil's advocate no matter what. By doing this, parents ensure that children develop a healthier sense of skepticism, the ability to analyze different perspectives, and repeated practice in thinking on their toes as they learn to justify their positions.

# Reaching Parents and Families

All of the parenting strategies in the world mean nothing if they never actually reach our parents. For educators and school leaders, nothing can be more frustrating than planning an amazing event for parents and seeing a poor turnout. After experiencing this frustration firsthand and working closely with schools and districts who have found a way to make their outreach work, I want to include some tips to help teachers provide access to these practical strategies for parents, who can then develop their children's critical thinking skills and dispositions.

First, shift the expectation of what it means to be an involved parent at your school. For so long, parent involvement has been limited to volunteering for the school carnival, selling popcorn to help with fundraising, and planning cool activities for Teacher Appreciation Week. But if our ultimate goal in education is to help all students unleash their full potential, is this the best use of parent volunteer hours? What if we asked our parents and families to play a more important role on the academic side?

I understand that workshop titles like "Helping Without Being Too Helpful" and "Encouraging Productive Struggle" may not exactly bring parents out in droves. But consider what kind of message it would send if your back-to-school night focused less on the calendar of fun events for the year and more on what parents can do to make this the best academic year of their children's lives. Imagine a carpool lane where, instead of receiving fliers to the next Panda Express fundraiser, parents received one practical strategy to practice that week for supporting critical thinking at home. Many teachers may believe that students' families are incredible assets in the academic success of students. But how will families know this if this message is so rarely communicated?

In addition to shifting the expectation of how parents can support academics, schools should rethink the parent workshop format as the sole means for delivering this information. Often, the parents we most want to show up to these events are the least likely to attend workshops. This could be because of work or home obligations, poorly timed workshops, or the sad reality that, for some families, going to their child's school can feel like returning to the scene of a crime. If parents have had an extremely negative experience in schools themselves, they are understandably hesitant to be involved.

However, families that are unlikely to attend workshops or read the school newsletters typically respond to and connect with their child's teacher, especially in elementary school. If teachers were to make "Encouraging Productive Struggle" a theme of the month and connect directly with families via text, phone calls, or in-person meetings to share a strategy a week, it is much more likely these lessons will reach families. Strategies like this can also be shared through your school's social media accounts to catch parents while they are scrolling through their timelines.

Meeting families where they are sometimes literally means *meeting them where they are.* Set up shop in a popular neighborhood area where students go trick-or-treating to hand out candy and share quick advice (like what to do when children ask parents a question they can probably answer on their own). I worked at a school that conducted mandatory home meetings for all families. I understand that this is not practical or even possible for all schools, but it was no surprise my school had standing room only at every parent event. Even though my school was in a neighborhood where surrounding schools had dismal attendance because, according to the explanations commonly provided by the administrative leaders of these surrounding schools, "these parents just don't care." You can tell families they are welcome. Or you can show them, which is significantly more powerful.

Lastly, if you are looking to implement traditional workshops, think about why parents do not attend them. I once had the idea of doing a Math Family Night when I taught in Washington, DC, and I was laughed out of my math team meeting. I was a first-year teacher, so I did not get the joke.

"Why wouldn't parents come?" I asked.

"Parents have to cook in the evening" the members of my team told me.

"Can't we just have some food?"

"Parents have to take care of their other children," they said.

"Can't they just bring their other children?"

"Half of these parents don't even speak English."

"Don't we have translators that work here?"

"They aren't going to come."

I asked, "What if we called every single one of them and asked them to come instead of assuming they won't show up?"

On the evening of our team's inaugural Math Family Night, I was extremely nervous. We had a very small setup in the library, and I did not know how it would go. But before we knew it, we had a packed house—so crowded, in fact, that we had to grab chairs from other classrooms. It turned out that the combination of being intentionally welcoming and creating a space for parents to learn alongside their children was uniquely appealing to families.

None of these tips for reaching parents is going to work in every situation. This is why it is helpful to know your families, their preferences on how they like to receive information, and what information they are really craving. Whatever strategy you use, remember the power of believing in parents as the incredible assets they are for their children's academic success and ensure that parents and families know that you truly believe in their power.

# Conclusion

*Future-Proofing Students with Critical Thinking*

I attended more than 250 education conferences across the United States in the nine years prior to publishing this book. One of the most common themes of these conferences was the "future of work." This is the idea that the 21st-century shift in the workforce involves a rate of transformation unlike anything we've ever seen. The urgent call to action, then, is to prepare our students for a highly flexible, super technological future if we want to avoid massive unemployment and economic crisis. One prominent doom-and-gloom keynote speaker put it this way: "If you can write an algorithm for your job, your job can be automated."

As a computer-science-graduate-turned-math-educator-turned-attorney-turned-critical-thinking-for-all advocate, my concerns are less dire but no less urgent. I'm less pessimistic because for every job wiped out because of technology, new ones are created. But my concerns are just as urgent because education leaders across the country are making a huge mistake in their well-intended desire to prepare students for the future of work: they are not prioritizing critical thinking as the key mechanism to create future-ready students.

Too many educators believe that if we just teach every student how to code, or if we just put every student in a career and technical education program, then somehow all students will be 21st-century ready. This is simply not true. I know this because lots of my fellow computer science

DOI: 10.4324/9781003482147-21

graduates were laid off in the last few years because knowing how to code without effective interpersonal skills isn't all that helpful in the real world. What tech companies really need are folks who can talk to tech geeks as well as buyers using the technology. I know this because I recognize that although certain technical certifications allow 19-year-olds to earn more than $70,000 a year, the rate of technological change moves quicker than it ever has. Why train students to do a specific job that may be high-paying today but obsolete in just a few years?

Our focus, therefore, cannot be coding for the sake of coding, or career and technical education for the sake of getting a job in a certain field. The focus must be broader and include what some dub "soft skills," like emotional intelligence, judgment, and—yes—critical thinking. This means that if we are teaching students to code, the lesson can't be just about learning how to code apps in Python. It must focus on learning how to listen to users about what their needs are, how to work in groups to communicate across lines of difference, and how to iteratively improve based on feedback. If we are training students to be certified in a technical field, the focus must be on building a transferable set of critical thinking skills, habits, and mindsets they can use to be problem solvers and problem finders in any context. These soft skills (which are probably the hardest to teach) are the difference-makers that separate us from the robots, and what we truly need to make our students irreplaceable leaders in the workforce of tomorrow.

So, let's not be afraid of the robots. Let's be afraid of teachers who are glued to the "what" and "how to" because they are scared to make the essential 21st-century shift to the "why" and "what if." Let's be afraid of the steep decline in college students pursuing degrees in the liberal arts, even though the humanities teach us to be human—teaching students the creative, contextual, and cognitive skills that cannot be replaced by machines. Most importantly, let's be afraid of an education system that continues to provide these essential future-ready skills to only the most elite students at the most elite schools because we are still treating critical thinking like a luxury good.

As author and pundit Fareed Zakaria (2015) noted in a powerful warning against our STEM obsession, "critical thinking is, in the end, the only way to protect American jobs" (para. 16). If critical thinking is our only hope, the success of our future workforce demands equitable access to meaningful critical thinking as a key educational priority for students in all grade levels and subject areas.

In the last two years, I have spoken at and sat in countless education conferences focused on the transformational impact of artificial intelligence (AI) in education. But considering the extreme value of critical thinking to preparing future-ready students, I think it is helpful to ask ourselves one last powerful, but practical question:

What if we are underestimating the power of the other AI? Actual Intellect?

Actual Intellect means I don't need to compete with large language models and machine learning that undoubtedly exceed human capacity to know all of the "what's" and "how-to's." Instead, young people need to know how to think about the "why's" and the "what-if's," how to learn, unlearn, and relearn, and how to listen, reason, persuade, collaborate, and influence others.

Just like technological shifts of the past, this isn't as simple as "AI will wipe out jobs." And it goes even further than the popular hand-wringing prediction amongst AI futurist experts that "people who know AI will wipe out the jobs of people who do not." It turns out that thinkLaw's obsession with critical thinking is a solid path towards future-proofing learners for whatever will come. The only way forward is to ensure we create a new educational reality, where critical thinking is no longer a luxury good. Thank you for being a part of this essential critical thinking revolution.

# Bibliography

Bloom, B. (Ed.). (1956). *Taxonomy of educational objectives: The classification of educational goals. Handbook I: Cognitive domain.* Longmans Green.

Bridgeland, J. M., DiIulio, Jr., J. J., & Morison, K. B. (2006). *The silent epidemic: Perspectives of high school dropouts.* Civic Enterprises.

CASEL. (2023, October 9). *Fundamentals of SEL.* https://casel.org/fundamentals-of-sel/

CBS News. (2015, October 7). Harvard debate team loses to New York prison inmates. *CBS News.* https://www.cbsnews.com/boston/news/harvard-debate-team-new-york-prison-inmates/

Coffey, M., & Tyner, A. (2023). *Excellence gaps by race and socioeconomic status.* Thomas B. Fordham Institute. https://fordhaminstitute.org/national/research/excellence-gaps-race-and-socioeconomic-status

Floyd, T. (2019, November 27). What happened after a team of prisoners beat Harvard in a debate. *The Hill.* https://thehill.com/changing-america/enrichment/education/472133-what-happened-after-a-team-of-prisoners-beat-harvard-in/

Green, A. (2017). Owners must surgically 'debark' loud dogs, court rules. *The Oregonian.* https://www.oregonlive.com/pacific-northwest-news/2017/08/owners_must_surgically_debark.html

Isadore, C. (2016). College coaches make more than players get in scholarships. *CNN Business.* https://money.cnn.com/2016/01/11/news/companies/college-coaches-pay-players-scholarships

Jimenez, L., Sargrad, S., Morales, J., & Thompson, M. (2016). *Remedial education.* Center for American Progress. https://www.americanprogress.org/issues/education-K–12/reports/2016/09/28/144000/remedial-education

King, Jr., M. L. (1947). The purpose of education. *The Maroon Tiger, 10,* 123–124.

King, M. L. (2018, April 5). *Address at the conclusion of the Selma to Montgomery March.* Retrieved December 12, 2019, from https://kinginstitute.stanford.edu/king-papers/documents/address-conclusion-selma-montgomery-march

Manfull, M. (2006, February 19). Slam Dunk: Robinson gets an assist from fellow little guy. *The Houston Chronicle.* https://www.chron.com/sports/rockets/article/Slam-Dunk-Robinson-gets-an-assist-from-fellow-1898634.php

National Collegiate Athletic Association. (2018). *NCAA recruiting facts.*https://www.ncaa.org/sites/default/files/Recruiting%20Fact%20Sheet%20WEB.pdf

National Governors Association Center for Best Practices, & Council of Chief State School Officers. (2010). *Common core state standards for mathematics.* NGA Center for Best Practices.

National Governors Association Center for Best Practices, & Council of Chief State School Officers. (2010). *Common core state standards for English language arts.* NGA Center for Best Practices.

NBC Sports. (2017, March 24). Video: Why did the NCAA ban dunking in 1967?. *NBC Sports.* https://www.nbcsports.com/college-basketball/news/video-why-did-the-ncaa-ban-dunking-in-1967

NCAA.org. (2014a). *Scholarships.* https://www.ncaa.org/sports/2014/10/6/scholarships.aspx#:~:text=NCAA%20Divisions%20I%20and%20II,scholarships%20to%20compete%20in%20college

Plucker, J. A., Hardesty, J., & Burroughs, N. (2013). *Talent on the sidelines: Excellence gaps and America's persistent talent underclass.* Center for Education Policy Analysis, University of Connecticut.

Ritchotte, J. A., & Graefe, A. K. (2017). An alternate path: The experience of high-potential individuals who left school. *Gifted Child Quarterly, 61*(4), 275–289. https://doi.org/10.1177%2F0016986217722615

Seale, C. (2022). 7 Tips for implementing and sustaining tangible equity priorities. In *Tangible equity: A guide for leveraging student identity, culture, and power to unlock excellence in and beyond the classroom* (pp. 92–102). Routledge.

Slobodkina, E. (1968). *Caps for sale: A tale of a peddler, some monkeys, and their monkey business.* HarperCollins.

Subramanian, C. (2016). Alvin Toffler: What he got right—and wrong. *BBC News.* https://www.bbc.com/news/world-us-canada-36675260

Suntex International Inc. (2019). *How to play.* https://www.24game.com/t-about-howtoplay.aspx

The Center for Depth and Complexity. (2024, January 17). *The depth and complexity icons.* https://depthcomplexity.com/the-icons/.

The Hewlett Foundation. (2013). *Deeper learning competencies.* https://hewlett
.org/wp-content/uploads/2016/08/Deeper_Learning_Defined__April_2013
.pdf

TNTP. (2018). *The opportunity myth: What students can show us about how school is letting them down—and how to fix it.* https://tntp.org/assets/documents/ TNTP_The-Opportunity-Myth_Web.pdf

Tyson, N. D. [NeilTyson] (2019, August 5). In the past 48hrs, the USA horrifically lost 34 people to mass shootings. On average, across any 48hrs, we also. *Twitter.* https://twitter.com/neiltyson/status/1158074774297468928

Webb, N. L. (1999). *Alignment of science and mathematics standards and assessments in four states.* National Institute for Science Education.

Wolverton, B. (2010). *NCAA agrees to $10.8-billion deal to broadcast its men's basketball tournament.* The Chronicle of Higher Education. https:// www .chronicle.com/article/NCAA-Signs-108-Billion-Deal/65219

Wyner, J. S., Bridgeland, J. M., & DiIulio, J. J. (2007). *Achievement trap: How America is failing millions of high-achieving students from lower-income families.* Jack Kent Cooke Foundation.

Zakaria, F. (2015). Why America's obsession with STEM education is dangerous. *Washington Post.* https://www.washingtonpost.com/opinions/why-stem-wont -make-us-successful/2015/03/26/5f4604f2-d2a5-11e4-ab77-9646eea6a4c7 _story.html

# About the Author

**Colin Seale** was born and raised in Brooklyn, NY, where struggles in his upbringing gave birth to his passion for educational equity. Tracked early into gifted and talented programs, Colin was afforded opportunities his neighborhood peers were not. Using lessons from his experience as a math teacher, later as an attorney—and now as a keynote speaker; contributor to *Forbes, The 74, Edutopia* and *Education Post*; and author of *Thinking Like a Lawyer: A Framework for Teaching Critical Thinking to All Students* (2020) and *Tangible Equity: A Guide for Leveraging Student Identity, Culture, and Power to Unlock Excellence In and Beyond the Classroom* (Routledge, 2022)—Colin founded thinkLaw (www.thinklaw.us), a multi-award-winning organization to help educators leverage inquiry-based instructional strategies to close the critical thinking gap and ensure they teach and reach all students, regardless of race, zip code, or what side of the poverty line they are born into. When he's not serving as the world's most fervent critical thinking advocate or tweeting from @ColinESeale, Colin proudly serves as the world's greatest entertainer to his two young children.